Coming Home

Coming Home

A Return Journey to Place and Self
Through the Iowa Woods

by Maureen Clarke

MILL CITY PRESS

Mill City Press, Inc.
2301 Lucien Way #415
Maitland, FL 32751
407.339.4217
www.millcitypress.net

Printed in the United States of America

ISBN-13: 9781545640203

We shall not cease from exploration,
And the end of all our exploring
Will be to arrive where we started
And know the place for the first time.

~ T.S. Eliot

Prologue

$\mathcal{I}$ gave the annoying mosquito a quick slap and then flicked its mangled body off my forearm with my middle finger. Score: Me – 3, Mosquitos –137. They were winning by a landslide.

I lifted the sweaty bottle of Michelob Ultra to my lips and took a long swallow in celebration of my small victory.

I set the bottle into the cup holder of my patriotic-patterned folding lawn chair and rose to stoke the campfire. A few pokes ignited the smoldering logs and bright orange and red flames danced again in the fire pit.

The evening air sent a rush of goose-bumps down my arms, so I retrieved a sweatshirt from my tent. It was early summer, the sun was bidding its farewell, and the stars were anxious to make their appearance. The songbirds' tunes were waning, gradually replaced by the soothing crescendo of the cicadas in the lush forest that surrounded me. A pair of white-tailed deer lingered nearby, and an owl hooted from a distant branch, signaling that bedtime was near.

I inched my chair a little closer to the bonfire and warmed my hands over its crackling heat. I took another long drink of my beer. Then I settled back and slowly became entranced by the fire's hypnotic glow.

Never in a million years could I have pictured myself here, camping alone, deep in the Iowa woods.

I just wasn't the type.

*"Blessed are the curious for they shall
have adventures."*

F reshly retired, I was desperate for an Adventure. A Big Adventure. A Big Lasting Adventure. But not a Big Lasting *Dangerous* Adventure. I was, after all, 58-years-old. I did not wish to hike the Appalachian Trail or climb Mount Everest. I just wanted to do something that would send me past my comfort zone but would not send me to my death.

This adventure had to include hiking, my passion, but not extreme hiking as I had a knee that needed replacement and a hip that needed a shot of cortisone. And my adventure had to be within my retirement budget.

But more important than the thrill of a new experience, I knew this escape would be a journey of healing.

I needed to recover from a career that left my soul wounded, my spirit defeated, and my self-worth shattered. I had to rescue the lively Iowa farm girl I once used to be.

Destination: Iowa

*T*he worst part about downsizing was that I knew there wouldn't be room for all my treasured books. They had been my companions when real-life relationships failed me throughout the years.

When I moved back to Iowa in 2016 after fifteen years in New England, I rented a stylish two-bedroom townhome in the expensive suburb of West Des Moines. But now, nine months later, I had decided that it was more important to spend my money on travel than rent. So, I was moving into a tiny 1926 cottage, a cute one-bedroom rental in the classic Waterbury area in Des Moines.

I set my stepladder against the tall bookshelves and climbed up to reach the stacks of books on top. I had started a 'keep' pile and a 'sell' pile. The 'sell' pile would be taken to the Half Price Bookstore to see what cash I could pocket.

The Happiness Project. Sell.

Feel the Fear and Do It Anyway. Sell.

How to Make Anyone Fall in Love with You. Sell. No, keep.

Then I came across two books that caught my attention. I had forgotten that I bought these books at Goodwill shortly after I returned to Iowa. I climbed down from the ladder, stepped over my piles, and carried the books to my computer chair where I sat down and began to flip through the pages. They were guides about hiking and walking trails in Iowa. I reached for my cheater glasses from the top of my desk and adjusted them on my nose to take a better look. Many of the trails looked beautiful and challenging. I was surprised.

A light bulb flicked to life above my head.

My adventure would be to hike Iowa! *Home*.

Time to Mull

*A*fter studying the guidebooks, I decided I wanted to hike the trails that traced the perimeter of the state. Now I had this tiny matter of lodging to consider.

Time wasn't a factor. I was retired and could devote the whole summer to this adventure. I just wanted to be back to Des Moines in time for the Iowa State Fair, which began mid-August.

Money, however, was.

I was used to comfort. Sometimes luxury. On my birthday one year, shortly after I moved to New Hampshire, I spoiled myself with a get-away at the luxurious Castle Inn in Newport, Rhode Island. It had an in-room Jacuzzi and fireplace, a private beach, and a private deck where I could watch the yachts sail in and out of the harbor. The cost was $500 per night. I stayed two.

I often escaped from my embittered career in New England by staying in lovely places on weekends. I pampered myself with charming bed and breakfasts overlooking the ocean, luxury cabins tucked into the White Mountains, and cozy inns on Acadia, but never did I check into a Motel 6.

Even if I stayed in the cheapest hotels during my adventure, it would still cost an arm and a leg. Plus, hotels were *boring*.

How could I afford this journey around the state?

I began to mull.

Me? Camping?

I stopped for gas after a day kayaking at Big Creek, a recreational park just north of Des Moines. As I filled up the tank, I happened to look up just in time to see the cutest little camper pass by. I had never seen anything like it before.

When I got home, I searched Craigslist for small campers, hoping I would find something that looked like what I had seen. I found one after a short search and discovered they were called 'teardrop' campers.

Okay, let's back the camper up here for a minute. What was I doing? A camper? Really? I had never been camping before – never even considered it. I'm all for outdoor activities: hiking is on top of my list, then kayaking, rollerblading, snowshoeing, ice skating, volleyball, and biking and tennis before my knee went bad.

But camping? No. I've never had the desire to 'rough it'. I was just too much of a sissy for camping life.

But this little camper was adorable and just my size! On my local Craigslist search, I found a used teardrop camper for sale for $5,000. Yikes. Or I could have one custom made starting at $12,000. Double yikes. I might as well stay in a cheap hotel. I wondered if my 4-cylinder jeep would even be able to pull one of these.

Then I thought about renting a small RV, but nixed this idea, sure this lodging option would be expensive. Plus, I didn't really want to drive one of those clumsy things.

Hmmm...

What about, dare I say, a...tent?

I shuddered at the thought.

A tent would be cheap.

It could be... fun?

No, I just wasn't the type.

And yet...

Time to Get Serious

I sat in my jeep in the Bass Pro Shops parking lot, waiting for my brother-in-law. He was going to help me pick out camping equipment. I knew that he was active in Cub Scouts with his young son Riley, and they went camping together often.

I had never been in a Bass Pro Shops store before. Judging by the gigantic, ugly fish on the outside of the building - let alone the name of the place - I had assumed that the Bass Pro Shops was just for avid fishermen.

Jeff assured me that they sold all sorts of outdoor equipment and that I would find everything I needed for my adventure here.

I arrived twenty minutes before our planned meeting time and mentally reviewed my list to bide my time until he arrived. I knew that I needed a tent although I didn't know what size. Something big enough to move around inside, I guessed. A sleeping bag to keep me warm at night. A small lantern to read by. This should be easy.

When I couldn't contain my excitement any longer, I decided to wait for Jeff inside the store. My heart was pumping faster than an Olympic sprinter when I opened the gigantic double doors.

Jeff was still wearing his Hy-Vee polo shirt with his silver name tag attached when he arrived. He gave me one of his big toothy grins and said, "Hi Po!"

"Po" is the shortened version of "Posey", the nickname my father gave me when I was a child. He said my rosy cheeks reminded him of the sweet flower. Whenever he called me Maureen instead of Posey, I knew I was in trouble. "Posey" has been modified into many different names from my siblings through the years, from "Pojo" to "Pojodo" to "PoDeODo".

Jeff had a small red notepad in one hand and a sharpened pencil in the other. "Let's sit over here so I can find out just what you want," he said.

He led me to the huge flannel-covered chairs that would make a pair of grizzly bears want to climb onto, curl up and hibernate. I told Jeff I was going to take off on an adventure in June. My plan was to explore the hiking trails in Iowa and stay in campgrounds along the way. The tiny problem was that I had never been camping before. I had never pitched a tent. I had never built a fire. And shit, I had never even pooped in a porta-pot. I admitted that my survival skills were, at best, non-existent.

I needed his help.

And, I asked him, would I be safe alone in the woods? I had lived alone all my adult life and had never been afraid. But this was different. Did I need to worry about a crazed predator ripping through my tent, slashing my throat, and then stealing my food?

Jeff looked at me and said with a grin, "Po, this is Iowa."

"What about thievery? Will I come back from a day of hiking and find my tent and everything in it gone? Is there some sort of 'code of honor' between campers?"

"Not to worry," Jeff said, amused.

I remembered that I had a cute, tiny padlock that I could use to secure my tent while I was gone during the day and to keep me safe at night.

"What about reservations? Would I need these?" I asked.

"Probably not, especially during the week," he said.

With this preliminary stuff out of the way, we nudged past the silver turnstile and into the massive showroom.

Walking down the main aisle (which seemed as wide as Interstate 235), we made our way past the flowing waterfall to the camping section.

Where to begin? With the tents, of course. I told Jeff that I wanted a tent large enough to move around in, so he suggested a four-man tent. I saw a tent with a screened-in porch that I thought was neat-o. This would keep the bugs from bothering me when I read in the evenings.

Next, a sleeping bag. Would I really need one of these flannel cocoons in the summer? Couldn't I just take my warm quilt? Jeff advised that the evenings still could get chilly. I liked the pretty blue and black plaid one: $80.00.

"What about a cot? That would be more comfortable for you than sleeping on the ground," Jeff said.

"Good point, especially with my bad knee. I would have a hard time getting up off the ground."

$39.99 for a folding cot. Not bad.

We continued systematically down the aisles, checking out all the equipment and gadgets. A small ax? "This would be good for splitting small branches for your fire," Jeff said. Then he picked up a machete. "And this may be what you need for protection out in the wild."

"You're teasing, right?" I gave him a sidelong glance.

"You should at least take a whistle," Jeff said. Good idea.

We bypassed the cooking area, as I told Jeff I wasn't planning on doing any grilling over the open fire. I wasn't much of a meat eater.

"What are you going to eat?" he asked.

"I haven't much thought about it."

"What do you eat for supper now, at home?"

"Usually a Weight Watcher's frozen entrée," I said. "I guess I can just forage for berries in the woods."

Jeff looked at me and just shook his head. He knew me too well.

I left the store with a four-man tent (I decided against the one with the screen. It would be just another thing to mess with in the assembly and also an added cost.), a can of waterproofer for my tent, a lantern, firesticks, matches, a cute teal mini clamp light, insect repellant, a whistle, and a cot. I had to return to the store to exchange the lantern for another model as I couldn't get the large battery compartment open due the arthritis in my right hand. I decided not to buy a sleeping bag, sure that a sweatshirt and my old quilt would keep me warm.

The Best Advice Ever

"*T*hat was simple," I said.

"Yep, nothing to it." Jeff had agreed to help me practice setting up my tent.

We clumsily assembled the tent in his living room, negotiating the folding poles around the furniture, while his wife, my sister, looked on. Her eyes said, "Why don't you do this outside?"

Their 11-year old son, Riley, bounded down the stairs and slipped into the open tent. He stretched his nimble body out onto the slick floor of the tent and then popped up again.

"Do you approve?" I asked.

He gave me a quick nod.

"Tell me, Riley, since you are a Cub Scout and have done a lot of camping: what's the best advice you can give me?"

Without hesitation, he said, "Don't get eaten by a bear."

Rough Road Ahead

I opened my crisp Iowa map and spread it across the wide oak table of the West Des Moines Library. It was a rainy Saturday morning, a perfect day to plan a rough itinerary of my adventure. I unpacked my two Iowa hiking books from my satchel along with an Iowa travel guide. Then I pulled up Pinterest on my laptop and entered 'Iowa' into the search box.

First, I researched hiking trails in Iowa. I was amazed to find so many. I knew I wanted to stay in campgrounds that either had hiking trails on the grounds or nearby. I also made a list of tourist attractions that I wanted to see along the way. Mostly, these were places around the perimeter of the state since I grew up in central Iowa.

The travel guide listed campgrounds in the state and noted whether they had modern shower facilities. I had to have a shower. I looked up the hiking trails, checked what campgrounds were nearby, and planned my route accordingly. I didn't want to stay more than three or four nights in any one campground as I had a lot of country to see. I was going to take my chances and not make any reservations. I wanted to be able to change my agenda at any time: stay longer in a place if I liked it, move on if I didn't.

I also set some rules for my adventure:

1. I could not take the Interstate, only backroads so I could really see the countryside.
2. I could not pack up my site and stay in a hotel unless tornado sirens were sounding.
3. I must hike every day.
4. I must limit my use of technology – no internet unless necessary.

I carefully folded up the map and put the books back into my satchel. I was as excited about this trip on my home soil as I had been about any vacation I had taken to foreign lands. It would be a journey like no other and I couldn't wait to hit the road.

Unplugged

I said farewell to my friends via social media by posting, "I'm going 'off the grid' for four to six weeks. No internet, no phone, no television. It may just be the best time of my life!"

As I rested my head upon my crisp cotton pillowcase the night before my adventure began, I became a little apprehensive about the journey that lay ahead of me. Would I be bored? Scared? Lonely? Would I realize that camping wasn't for me and be pulled back to the comforts of my life?

And was I really willing to give up *Judge Judy* and *Rachel Maddow* for an extended period of time?

But I had made this commitment to myself and I knew in my heart that no matter how uncomfortable this trip would be, I would stick with it.

What was the worst that could happen? I thought, as I snuggled deeper into my warm bed. *A snake in my tent?*

Yeah, that would be pretty bad.

Day 1

*A*nd so the adventure begins!

I kicked off my blankets and jumped out of bed at 6:00 a.m., as excited as a kid on Christmas morning. I took a quick shower and packed all my equipment and supplies into the back of my jeep. I checked and re-checked my list. Since I had never been camping before, it would be a test to see what I used and what I'd forgotten to buy.

Finally, I jumped in behind the wheel. I took a deep breath, put my jeep in reverse, and pulled out of the parking lot of my apartment building. I was on my way.

True to my rules (no Interstate), I made my way onto University Avenue, which eventually turned into Highway 163. This highway would lead me to southeast Iowa, the beginning of my journey. Traffic was light at 7:00 in the morning.

What memories this stretch of road held for me. I first passed Drake University, my alma mater. What a beautiful campus. I attended night classes there for three years and received my BS in Psychology in 1989.

Mercy Hospital loomed next, where my father passed away in 1993. I didn't witness his death, which was both a blessing and a sorrow.

The Mail Processing Plant for the Postal Service, where I worked for years, was across the street from the hospital. That's where I met and lost the love of my life. *Tragic*. Enough said.

I knew the next landmark along Highway 163 would be bittersweet for me: the farmstead where I was raised. The happiest days of my life were spent on this treasured piece of land. I couldn't remember the last time I'd been by the place, so I had no idea what to expect.

Highway 163 had developed into a busy four-lane thoroughfare in recent years due to commuter traffic to and from Des Moines. When my father grew up in the farmhouse, it was part of a community - a scattered handful of homesteads called Fairmont. This tiny rural town then boasted a general store and a grain elevator. Now, Fairmont doesn't appear on any map. When I googled it, Fairmont, Minnesota kept popping up. Finally, after persistent searching, Fairmont, Iowa appeared as a red teardrop shape indicating a location between Prairie City and Monroe.

Back then, our traditional four-square white farm-house sat alone on the one-mile gravel road that led past it. Hidden by a cluster of mature oak trees, the house was surrounded by soybean and corn fields. We lived on the farm until 1967, when we sold the house and land and built a house in Colfax, the town where my mother taught school and we attended the catholic church.

I searched along the highway for the two strong oak trees that had always been the beacon for us. As children, when the five of us could see the familiar silhouettes of those trees from our station wagon, we knew we were close to home.

It soon occurred to me I'd gone too far and so I turned around. I was saddened by the realization that those beautiful trees had been cut down. That's why I missed the turn. They were no longer there to signal me home.

Sheltered under those trees, our mailbox had stood next to our neighbor's box. Those were gone too, probably moved in front of the houses now. I remembered walking barefoot the half mile to get our mail with my sisters in the summertime, arms linked, giggling as we dodged the fuzzy orange and black caterpillars creeping across the gravel road.

I spotted the street signs that pointed to our farm: "S 96th Ave W" and "Dead End". I turned down the road I'd so often traveled in my youth. I stopped midway to retrieve my camera from the back of my jeep. Then I shifted back into gear and slowed as the house came into view.

I stopped in the road, got out of my jeep, and slowly took in the peaceful homestead before me. The house was no longer white but painted a soft tan. The screened-in porch, where we would sit on the swing on hot summer nights and listen to the rhythmic strumming of cicadas, had been enclosed.

A satellite dish stood out of place among the apple trees on the left side of the house. The two young elm trees in the front yard that we tirelessly climbed had matured and shaded the lawn that seemed to have become much smaller since my youth.

Whispers of my childhood swirled around me and I fought back the tears of a remembered past.

I saw the ghost of my father playing work-up baseball with us in the yard after supper. He hit the ball and we playfully pulled him around the bases by his calloused hands.

I saw a vision of my mother plucking white sheets from the clothesline. A brisk breeze slapped her plain farmer's dress around her bare legs. Our collie, Lassie, danced in circles behind her.

I stood in the middle of the gravel road, desperate to return to my life as the barefoot girl with skinned knees and freckles. I wanted to dress up my cats in doll clothes and play "Mother, May I" with my brother and sisters. I wanted to hop out of the Bookmobile that had parked in our driveway, hugging an armful of books in my arms. I wanted to sleep in homemade seersucker pajamas. I wanted to accompany my mother as she took a thermos of coffee and a slice of apple pie to my father in the fields in the middle of the afternoon.

My heart ached for a time and place that I could never recapture.

The German Shepard that had been napping on the concrete porch steps growled and came closer as I aimed my camera. I hesitated. Then I eased the cap back on the lens and returned it to its case. I wanted to remember this house from the precious images that I had tucked away in a special place in my heart.

Reluctantly, I took one last look at the place I loved so much. I turned my jeep around and drove back to the highway. When I slowed to the stop sign, I removed my sunglasses, swallowed hard, and dabbed a tissue at my wet lashes. Then I made a left turn back onto Highway 163.

The first stop on my adventure was where it all began.

Soon, Monroe Elementary School came into view. I attended this school until the 5th grade when we moved to Colfax. I barely gave the single-story red brick building a second glance as I passed. My days here were painful and lonely as I suffered from severe shyness.

On my first day of kindergarten, I remember hiding behind my mother's skirts when she presented me to my teacher and the frightening world beyond the farm.

In 1st grade, my teacher, Mrs. Hugan, made me stay in from recess because I refused to talk in class. In fact, I used to hide my head in the lift-up desk. This may be why one side of my head is rather flat. My shyness was so bad that Mrs. Hugan once sent a note home to Mother. As Mother tried to talk to me about it that evening, I cowered behind our big green chair, howling, and declared that I was never going back to 'that school' again!

Mrs. Hugan had sort of a one-on-one 'show and tell' minus the 'show' in her class. Every afternoon, students could line up and tell her something fascinating. Of course, I was too timid to ever participate. Well, after that horrifying note, one day I mustered up my courage, got in line, and whispered to Mrs. Hugan that "I saw the clouds move." I strutted back to my desk with my chest all puffed out!

On the last day of school, Mrs. Hugan lined up all her students. She shook hands with all the boys and kissed all the girls on the cheek. When she got to me, she bent down and whispered in my ear, "Now Maureen, you have to promise me that you won't be so shy in the second grade." I looked down at my toes and nodded.

The next year she found me sitting alone on the playground and gently scolded, "Maureen, you broke your promise."

Another thirty minutes and I was passing through Pella and Central College. Another lovely campus. I went here for two years just out of high school. I would have completed my college education here if I'd had a clue what I wanted to do with my life. I tried an Elementary Education program as my Mother was a teacher and my two older sisters were following in her footsteps. It didn't take me long to figure out I wasn't born for this profession.

I continued my drive toward southeast Iowa, pulling off the highway often to snap photographs of ramshackle barns and sheds. I felt I had something in common with these old dilapidated buildings: I had weathered storms,

I was aged, my beauty lost, and I sagged in places. But I was still standing!

Outside of Pulaski, I met several Amish buggies plodding along the side of the two-lane highway, the horses' hooves rhythmically clip-clopping on the pavement as I passed. So simple, so *Iowa*.

I headed for Lacey-Keosauqua State Park, where I would be camping for the next two nights. According to my hiking book, this park had some good hiking trails. My body screamed for some strenuous exercise after having spent all morning driving. Since I didn't have a reservation, I assumed that I couldn't check into the campground until 3:00.

I drove to the far end of the park and saw a metal posted sign with a brown hiker man clutching a walking stick on it. I would come to love this brown hiker man.

As I pulled into the parking area, I noticed a strong smell of gas in my jeep. *Just great*. I thought. *My jeep breaks down on the first day of my adventure! Is this a sign that I should be home watching Judge Judy?*

I had noticed an auto shop when I'd driven through town on the way here. Should I skip the hike and call the shop? Damn. Damn. Damn.

Then something occurred to me. The can of water-proofer I'd bought to spray on my tent once I had it set up had a loose cap. Could the cap have come off and leaked?

I got out of my jeep, lifted my tailgate and checked the basket where I'd stored the can along with some other equipment. The cap had come off completely, and the weight from supplies on top of it had set off the nozzle and it had sprayed all over. The cotton lining of the basket was soaked. It did smell like gas.

Thank goodness I'd checked this before I made a fool of myself at the auto shop. My quilt, pillow, and cot had also been in the line of fire. It was going to take a while for them to air out. At least I could toss the liner of the basket so my jeep wouldn't smell so bad. I decided to deal with this issue later and do some hiking.

I loaded up my backpack, strapped on my knee brace, and set off on the first trail of my adventure. It had some steep climbs, but it was rather boring. I wanted something with some views. The mosquitos were relentless, but I was expecting a few bites on this adventure.

It was still early in the afternoon when I finished this uneventful hike, so I decided to check my guidebook for another trail within the park. The book highlighted a trail just across the road, the River Trail. I set off on this roller-coaster trail, my gait in rhythm with the songs of the birds in the treetops. I came to a deserted picnic area about midway through the trail and decided to stop a while to rest.

I dropped my trekking stick, shrugged off my backpack, and sat down on a green paint-chipped picnic table. A quartet of red-winged blackbirds darted out of the trees and took flight over the lazy Des Moines River. A soft breeze cooled my cheeks, rewarding me for my excursion. I closed my eyes, lifted my face to the June sun, and basked in its warmth.

My thoughts automatically shifted, and I felt my carefree mood begin to lessen. I had been retired for nine months now, yet the wounds to my self-esteem I suffered during my career were still open and bleeding.

For so many years I had been blindly bumping through my days like a mindless pinball game, trapped in a job that held no meaning for me, and surrounded by people who still made me tremble when I thought of them. Although I could have worked much longer, I knew that I couldn't go on. I was too damn miserable, and life was too damn short. I hoped that immersing myself in nature on this sojourn would provide me with the medicine I so needed to heal.

My reverie was interrupted when a thirty-something woman pulled up in a punky-sized car, got out, and seated herself at a picnic table not far from where I sat. She stared off into space, just like I was doing. I wondered what her story was, if it was anything like mine.

Then she started to pick her nose, at which point I ceased to care.

I so wanted to continue with the hike, but decided to return to my jeep, as I needed to get checked into the campsite. I was a little nervous about everything, with this being my first night camping.

I went into town to buy food to take back to the campsite for supper which consisted of a single-sized serving of nacho chips and guacamole. Oh, and beer. The convenience store clerk told me they were out of firewood. Oh no! My first night camping and I couldn't have a bonfire! Tragic! How sad it would be to sit around a fire pit with no fire. Then she said that she was sure that the campground sold firewood.

I entered the campground precisely at 3:00, pulled up to the registration booth, and got out of my jeep. I looked at the mass of information posted on the board for several minutes. Huh? None of it made any sense to me. Camping was like a test that I didn't study for.

I must have looked really confused, because the campground host immediately stepped out of his RV, which was parked next to the booth. He was 60ish, short and firm, and had a smile as warm as his eyes. I liked him immediately.

"Hi," I said as he approached. "I've never camped before." I'm sure I was stating the obvious.

He showed me the registration form and explained how to complete it. "Then insert your money and drop the envelope in the chute." I was the only tent camper and there were just one or two other campers in the park. He gave me a site number but told me I could have any one I wanted since there most likely wouldn't be any other campers coming.

He introduced himself as LeRoy and patiently explained what to do with the site copy of the registration form. I was so glad that that this gentleman made my first experience camping so easy.

And yay! He sold firewood! He loaded up the back of my jeep with a generous supply of logs for $5.00.

I selected a site at the furthest spot on the tent loop. It was secluded, quiet, and bordered the woods. I set up my tent for the first time, as Jeff had taught me, and with little trouble. I stood back and admired my work. It was like how I felt when I'd successfully connected my DVD player to my cable television.

I broke a fire stick into three pieces and placed them strategically under a mound of twigs I had collected from the edge of the woods. They ignited immediately and soon I had a nice fire going. This camping stuff wasn't so hard!

I dined on the chips and guacamole I'd purchased earlier and twisted the cap off a cold Michelob Ultra. I toasted to the first night of my adventure as I settled into my lawn chair. There was no one around. This was my small pocket of the universe.

I had brought along a basketful of books to keep me entertained in the evenings. I decided to start out with *Thoreau's Journal*. After a few pages, I decided his thoughts were just too deep for me, so I tossed the book aside for something lighter and scandalous: *Peyton Place*.

It wasn't long before cicadas began their chanting, an echo from my childhood that I so missed. The last rays of sunlight slanted through the tall trees that hugged my campsite and nightfall gently pressed in around me. A firefly winked. The red and orange flames of the fire were dancing wildly as if to join me in celebrating my crazy escape.

I closed my eyes and felt embraced by the rhythms of nature surrounding me. Quietly, some of the heavy, lingering despair from my past life slipped from my soul.

I let the logs disintegrate into smoldering embers before I reluctantly decided that it was time to end the first day of my adventure. I unzipped my tent and crawled onto my cot. I lit my lantern and continued to read for a little while. Then my iPhone chimed, and the screen showed a text from Jenny, one of my best gal-pals from my volleyball days.

"Are you still taking calls?" She was referring to the sign-off I'd posted on Facebook before I'd left on my adventure.

I called her back immediately and filled her in on how things were going so far. As soon as I got her on the phone, I heard a critter rummaging just outside my tent. I remembered that I had left a garbage bag out there with the empty guacamole container. It was probably just a raccoon. Those bandits didn't scare me. Anything larger, well, that would be a different story.

I told Jenny about the gas incident in my jeep and how it still smelled. Her suggestion? I needed to just "let one rip" - that should cover the smell. One gas smell to disguise another?

"Jenny," I blurted out. "I had four beers tonight!"

"You said that like it was a bad thing," Jenny teased.

Jenny and I have been known to go into a bar and sit and chat for four or five hours and never run out of things to talk about. I love that about her. She lives out of state, so we don't see each other very often, but when we get together we just pick up where we left off.

We soon ended the conversation, but not before promising to meet for corn dogs at the Iowa State Fair in August.

What I learned today: You can't go home again.

~ ~ ~

I often wonder what my life would have been like if I'd stayed at the small post office in my home town, where I was hired because I looked, according to the postmaster, "sturdy." I could have spent my career delivering mail, with no greater strain on my brain than "this letter goes in this box". I liked when customers on my route met me at their doors with fresh lemonade in the humid summers and steaming cocoa in the frigid winters. I also would have been spared the harassment and discrimination that I suffered in my postal career that spanned thirty-eight years.

But the promise of more hours, and thus more money, lured me to the Mail Processing Plant in Des Moines. This is where all the trouble began.

Within a year, I was the successful candidate for a low-level position in the Marketing Department. I applied, thinking it would be a good way to get my foot in the door. Plus, it was an escape from the junior-high school mentality of the personnel on the work-room floor. Rumor had it that I got the job because I had slept with my new boss. I had never even met him until I was hired.

Whenever this boss (I'll call him Bob) needed something from the Plant Manager for one of our business customers, he required that I attend the meeting between the two of them. He was convinced that his chances of obtaining the favor were much greater if I was along. He told me to just "sit in my chair and look pretty."

Day 2

*W*ell, that didn't go so well.

I spent the first night of my adventure in my jeep. Not sleeping in my jeep. Just in my jeep. There was a difference.

I knew my cot wouldn't be as comfortable as my soft, warm mattress, but darn it if I didn't toss and turn and toss and turn, then toss and turn some more. There is not much room to toss and turn on a fold-up cot. Maybe my sleep was hindered by the shooting pain in my hip due to that stupid bursitis. I wished I'd gotten a cortisone shot before taking off on this adventure.

I had tried reciting the rosary on the beads Mother had made for me. Usually I'm asleep by the third decade of Hail Marys (Mother always said that if you fall asleep saying the rosary, the angels will finish it for you.). Finally, I dozed off and woke at 1:30 to the cracking of twigs outside of my tent. My teeth were chattering, but I didn't know if it was because I was freezing or because I was terrified of what creature lurked on the other side of my tent. I thought that my old tattered quilt would be warm enough. I was wrong.

I just couldn't stand the cold any longer and yearned for the warmth of my jeep. After a while, I couldn't hear any noises from outside my tent, so I figured that the critter or monster or alien had returned to its cave. I grabbed my quilt, my pillow, and my cute little teal flashlight. I unzipped the tent and rushed to my jeep.

There was no room for me in the back, as it was full of supplies and my cooler was on the floor of the passenger side. It would be too heavy to move from inside the jeep. And I wasn't going to make any adjustments from the outside while critters were lurking about. I was just going to have to maneuver my body around the steering wheel and my feet around the gas and brake pedals.

I reached in the back for a sweatshirt and pulled it on. I gathered my quilt around me, punched my pillow, and curled up. It was going to be a long night.

Brilliant slants of sunlight through the trees woke me at 6:40 a.m. I Googled the nearest Walmart on my iPhone so I could buy a flannel sleeping bag for the rest of my journey. Fairfield was just 20 minutes away.

I tripped out of my jeep and tried to straighten my stiff body. My bones cracked and creaked. This must be how the Tin Man from The Wizard of Oz felt. I either needed a can of WD-40 or a hot shower.

I drove the few hundred yards to the restroom/ shower. My bladder was so full from my celebration the previous night that there was no way I could make the walk without leaving a smelly trail.

I pulled back the curtain on the first shower stall and scratched my head. I pulled back the curtain on the second shower stall and scratched my head. I pulled back the curtain on the third shower stall and scratched my head. All three showers were obviously broken. There were no shower knobs, just funny buttons on the wall. What now? LeRoy! Help!

Okay, I can figure this out. I twisted the button on the wall. Nothing. Then I pushed it. And magically, water came out. But not a continuous stream. I would have to keep pushing it every few minutes. But at least the water was hot - well, sort of. It was a far cry from my steamy, steady shower at home. I stripped down and pushed the button. Then again. Then again. Sigh. I might as well get used to this.

After my shower, I took off for Fairfield, wanting to get the shopping out of the way so I could spend the rest of the day hiking. The smell of gas lingered in my jeep.

I paid just $17.99 for the sleeping bag. The pretty plaid one at the Bass Pro Shops had been $80.00. This one was flannel-lined and sure to keep me warm. I did not want to spend another night in my jeep.

I took my time driving back, stopping to take photographs of anything that interested me: a small roadside graveyard, a broken windmill, a new foal with its mother. These were roads I had never travelled before. Rich beauty met me around every bend and I was mesmerized.

I drove through Farmington in search of county road F56, which would bring me to a trailhead for a hike through the Shimek State Forest. According to my hiking guidebook, F56 was a left (east) turn off Highway 2. It looked like it was just on the outskirts of town, judging by my map. I drove back and forth on Highway 2 searching and searching for a sign that said F56. Where in the hell was it? I consulted the hiking book and my Iowa map so many times I felt dizzy. Finally, I gave up.

Defeated and disappointed for spending over an hour searching for this trail, I headed back to the

Lacey-Keosauqua Park and the hike that I'd enjoyed so much the day before, the River Trail. I wanted to go the distance, all 9.5 miles round trip.

Feeling energetic, I meandered along the trail, the pace of my steps and the click of my hiking stick beating out a steady rhythm. Birds carried on lively conversations in the treetops above. I inhaled the woodsy smell and thought of one of my favorite quotes from Thoreau, "I returned to the woods where I am better known". I felt so at home.

There was eventually a break in the trees and I glimpsed the end of the trail, the Keosauqua Bridge. It was so far off in the distance that I was sure it would take me until the end of time to reach it. And I'd promised Jenny that I would be home in time for the State Fair. I reluctantly turned around and returned to my jeep, huffing and puffing and smiling.

I drove to the beach after I finished the hike. It was around 4:00 and the air had a refreshing coolness to it. I brought a beach chair and *Peyton Place* to read.

Three exasperated adult females and a boisterous cackle of kids were just clearing out when I arrived. A couple was sitting on the grassy bank next to where I had planted my chair, engaged in a really boring conversation. I was glad to have the characters of *Peyton*

Place to entertain me. The only people in the water were a mother with her young daughter, who was learning to swim.

Back at my campsite, I realized I must have set up my tent a little too close to the fire pit. I spotted a small hole where an aggressive spark from the night before must have flown through the air and burned through the tent. I made a mental note to set up my tent a little further back from the fire pit in the future.

Nut Thin crackers and guacamole for supper. Two beers to wash it all down. I wondered whether I would become a bona fide alcoholic by the end of this adventure.

What I learned today: County Road F56 does not exist and should be removed from all Iowa maps.

Day 3

What was that?!

I bolted upright, and forgetting I was cocooned in my pretty new blue and black plaid sleeping bag, rolled off my cot and onto the hard ground. Ouch!

It was a rasping, hissing noise coming from outside my tent, one like I had never heard before, not even in the most terrifying monster movies.

It belonged to a green, wart-covered, fire-breathing, one-eyed beast. I was sure of it. There was no way that I was going to unzip the flap of my tent to see what was out there.

Hissss…Hissss…

I waited. And listened.

Finally, the monster appeared to have retreated to its hollow in the woods.

The new sleeping bag made a difference. I had been sleeping so well until I heard the rasping. It was early in the morning and I was pumped for a full day of hiking.

After a quick shower (as quick as one can have in a campground), I was ready to hit the road. Destination: Starr's Cave Park and Preserve near Burlington.

As I drove out of the park, an idiot light on my dashboard lit up. Now what? I was sure it was my 'check engine' light. This couldn't be happening! Should I stop in at the local service station and see if they could take it in today? Or should I ignore it? Sometimes 'check engine' means nothing. On my VW Cabrio I had a few years ago, that stupid light wouldn't come off for months so I finally put a strip of duct tape over it so it wouldn't continue to annoy me.

One thing was certain: I did not want to waste the day sitting in a dusty service station waiting room reading Popular Mechanics magazines.

I pulled open my glove compartment and retrieved the owner's manual. It wasn't the 'check engine' light after all - it was the tire pressure light. That was an easy fix. I pulled up to a convenience store, bought 50 cents worth of air, and filled my front right tire to the suggested pressure level.

Then I hit the road.

I hate bats. In my memory lives a story my mother told me about my grandmother collecting laundry from the clothesline when Mother was a child. Bats flew down from the dusky sky and one lodged itself in Grandmother's wiry hair. None of my siblings remember hearing this story, yet it remains fixed in my mind, and I think of it every time I see or think of a bat.

Early in my hike at Starr's Cave Park, I walked across a bridge to a cave only to find that it was chained and locked up. The attached sign said it had been closed since 2010 due to White Nose Syndrome, or WNS. WNS is a disease that affects bats that hibernate in the winter and was named for the white fungus that grows on the bats' muzzles. The cave would be closed indefinitely to prevent the spread of this disease within the bat population.

Knowing that the cave housed bats, I wouldn't have gone in, even if it was open. I didn't want a bat to get stuck in my hair.

The hike here was strenuous and enjoyable, but it wasn't marked. I always feel wary about not being able to find my way back on a strange path when there are numerous junctions that lead to other trails. The hikes in New England had brightly colored blazes on the trees, so they were usually easy to follow.

As I returned to the parking lot after a couple of hours on this trail, two large groups of children with a couple of adult chaperons were playing in the grass on the side of the Nature Center. Shrieks and laughter and running and tumbling. And the kids were having fun too.

It was mid-day when I set off to Geode State Park, where I would be camping for the next three nights. With plenty of sunlight left, I got onto a trail within the park, a wonderful walk in the woods, but I lost the trail at a picnic area. There was a sign posted that had an arrow pointing to the trail's continuation. I searched all around the parking lot for the re-entry point into the woods but couldn't find anything. I stood in the lot, bewildered. It reminded me of searching for my car in the parking lot after leaving the grocery store. I just know it's gotta be here somewhere...

I registered at the campground and got my tent set up early. Then I went down to the beach. It was just nice to relax under a shade tree and read after a couple of exhausting hikes.

I just love to see kids at the beach. Their little legs move so fast, skittering through the sand like sandpipers. They run in and out of the water and squeal with such innocent delight. If ever I need cheering up, I just need to go to a beach and watch little ones at play.

Maybe I love this so much because I've never had children of my own.

Darn. I was out of beer. How did that happen? I decided to drive to Denmark, the closest town, and get a six-pack.

The campground was quiet when I got back: just a group at the end in a condo-tent and a family across from me in the tent section. Even though I relished the isolation, it was nice to have neighbors. Hopefully a gathering of campers would keep the critters at bay.

What I learned today: They are called 'idiot lights' for a reason.

Day 4

*M*y alarm clock, the singsong of birds, went off at 6:40. I put my contacts in, pulled on my hiking clothes, and tugged a cap over my unruly curls. I was on my way to Wildcat Den State Park in Muscatine.

I estimated that it would take more than an hour to get to Wildcat Den. I rolled the windows down and deeply inhaled the promise of a new day. It was the kind of morning that I wanted to bottle up and display on my shelf of favorite things.

I realized I had become a 'Sunday Afternoon' driver. I was spending more time gazing at the picturesque countryside around me than the road in front of me. I looked into my rearview mirror and imagined the motorists behind me cursing as they waited impatiently for a safe time to pass.

I arrived at the trail mid-morning and quickly reviewed the maps from my guidebooks. I completed my routine hiking prep and anxiously walked toward the familiar brown hiker man sign.

This was a tough hike, but so unique that it left me awestruck. The Devil's Punchbowl portion was incredible. It included multiple series of wooden steps that led to perfectly placed overlooks. This trail would be dazzling in the fall.

Why didn't I bring a map with me? I got confused past the Punchbowl and didn't want to get lost, so I turned around and retraced my steps. Then I tried another way but lost the trail at a picnic area. Why do I always seem to lose trails at picnic areas? Where oh where was my brown hiker man when I needed him?

When I got back to my jeep and looked at the maps, I discovered the error of my ways, but I knew I didn't have the energy to try again. I estimated I had already hiked a good three or four miles. And my knee was telling me, "enough already!"

I stopped at Walmart as I drove through town. My knee completely went out as I reached for a bunch of ripe bananas. I thought I was going to have to beg the grey-haired greeter to forfeit his wheelchair to me. Sometimes if I cross my knee wrong or twist it funny when I stand up, it goes all spastic on me. Still, I was going to put off the dreaded "replacement" for as long as I could.

When I returned to the park, I drove straight to the beach. I just wanted to soak in the cool water and let my knee work itself out.

The temperature had climbed to 90-degrees by the time I coaxed my bathing suit over my clammy skin. The wet sand felt so good between my toes. I splashed around in the water for a while, shook myself off like a dog, and then got comfortable on my beach chair, book in tow.

A twenty-something guy walked by wearing a fur-lined cap - one of those with ear-flaps that tie below the chin. Seriously? He looked prepared for a nor'easter. Granted, it was quite windy, so much so that a kayaker flipped over moments ago, but I was confident that snow was not in the forecast. My scalp prickled with sweat just looking at him.

It was early evening and the gray clouds were promising a storm when I returned to my site and got a fire started in the pit. I still had this section of the campground to myself and was relishing the quiet when a small red car with two bicycles attached to its rear bumper pulled in and parked across the road from me. A young man got out, his gray sweat pants pushed up to his knees. His pre-teen daughter jumped out of the passenger side. He quickly set up a red tent a quarter the size of mine. How could they possibly both fit in that?

Before long, the man came over to me and asked if I had a pen he could borrow. With his camper registration form in his hand, he went to the next picnic table and sat down. I could see him reading through the form and looking as confused as I had on Day One. His pig-tailed daughter skipped around him, restless, and he kept telling her to leave him alone.

Soon, he came back and asked for help with the form. Pro that I now was, I reviewed the registration process with him. I could see a campground host position in my future.

What I learned today: A one-piece bathing suit is impossible to tug on in 90-degree weather, especially if your body is still sweaty from a four-mile hike.

~ ~ ~

The newly appointed postmaster was making the rounds and introducing himself when I was an Account Representative in the Marketing Department in Des Moines. I could primp myself by looking down at the shine on his bald dome. I guessed from his jumbo ears and big front teeth that he had been bullied as a child.

He never made eye contact with me - just a creepy leer - as he shook my hand. I felt like covering myself as he checked me out from my legs to my bosom.

Shortly after he'd settled in to this new job, he phoned me and asked me to report to his office. What? The postmaster just doesn't call a low-level Account Representative. If there was a customer issue, he would need to go through the chain of command: first the Marketing Manager and then my boss, the Account Manager.

I arrived with my pen and notebook in hand, as I had no idea what he wanted. He was telling his secretary to hold all calls. Oh, no.

He motioned me into his office and shut the door. Then he asked me to sit on the couch and he made himself comfortable next to me. Well, as comfortable as he could, considering his feet didn't reach the floor. After a bit of small talk, we stood and he proudly showed me all the photographs on the walls which depicted his executive career in the Postal Service. I couldn't have cared less, but I feigned interest.

Then he faced me, took my clammy hands in his stubby ones and told me he wanted to take me out for coffee some night. He told me to call him in the next few days to arrange this. I thought: *This man is married. This man is the postmaster. This man should know better.*

I somehow made it back to my office, confused and angry. I was up for a promotion and he would have to sign off on it. Should I report this incident to my manager? If I didn't call him as requested, would I lose my shot at the promotion?

My brother-in-law advised me not to make the call and to report the incident to my manager. I took his advice, but my manager was not supportive or alarmed. Surprisingly, I did receive the promotion.

A few weeks later, the postmaster called me out of my office, and in the hallway, where anyone could have overheard our conversation, asked why I didn't call him as he'd asked me to. I told him that his request made me uncomfortable. He made no further advances toward me.

Day 5

I decided that my next hike would be Brinton Timber, near the town of Brighton, which would be an hour drive or so, but I had all day.

True to my directionally-challenged nature, it took me awhile to find the timber. I finally pulled into the parking lot mid-morning, and set off, full of energy and vigor. It was another beautiful Iowa summer day. I had been blessed with perfect hiking weather so far.

My guidebook said that the timber contained six different loops, all named and labeled with colored symbols painted on the trees. *Great,* I thought. *I wouldn't get lost on this trail.*

I decided to tackle the Wood Duck Trail first. Cute blue ducks were painted on the trees to mark the way. The path was sandy for a while, making the walking difficult. This reminded me of playing sand volleyball in my younger days. I was getting a good workout, and my thighs and calves felt it.

The path changed into a mix of gravel and rock and before long, I tripped and fell. I'm just plain clumsy. I have a two-inch scar on my right forearm from a tumble I took on a trail in Oregon last April. A few years ago, I broke my foot when I was still in a boot recovering from another broken bone in the same foot. I even managed to tumble once on a golf course green by tripping over my putter. Sigh...

I soon came across a posted sign that said the Wood Duck Trail was 1.5 miles. I was still pumped with energy, as this trail was mostly flat. I felt ready for more of a challenge, so I turned onto the Bent Rock Trail, a blue half-moon blaze, and pushed on. I crossed gurgling creeks by stepping on large stones, waking frogs from their slumber. The walking was getting tougher now and my pace wasn't quite so spry.

Still, when I saw the wooden post that said that the Tall Timber Trail was only 0.6 miles, I thought I could surely do that too. This trail, a level walk among tall timbers, went on and on and on and on. Had I read the sign wrong? Had it said 6 miles instead of 0.6 miles? Did I need to get my vision checked?

After what seemed like a week, I came to a sign that pointed to the Crazy Horse Trail loop. I was too pooped to loop, so I took the trail that led me back. I least I thought it was the trail that led me back.

The next sign I stumbled across had a map that said, "Red Arrow indicates your location." What red arrow? There was no red arrow! Help.

By this time, I was staggering along the path like some drunk who couldn't find his way home. I had to check my map against the posted signs and retrace my steps several times before I felt confident I was on the right path back.

When I finally spotted my jeep in the parking lot through the trees, I wanted to leap for joy. I would have, had I the energy. All the celebration I could muster was to raise my heels a smidge off the ground and mutter a faint, "Yay."

I pulled a cold bottle of Diet Pepsi from my cooler and drank it in one gulp. Even though the hike had been much more than I'd been prepared for - or even wanted - I was glad to have done it.

My tire pressure light was back on, so I found a Casey's General Store in Mt. Pleasant and put more air into the tire. I noticed a tire business next door that fixed tires, so I pulled in. The sign on the door said that they closed at noon on Saturday. It was Saturday, wasn't it? I glanced at the clock on the dashboard. 12:17. Damn.

It was getting unbearably hot. Thank goodness there was a strong wind. I was worried about not having secured my tent to the ground. What was the worst that could happen? I'd find it in the woods when I returned to the campsite? Or that I wouldn't find it in the woods when I returned to the campsite?

When I got back to the campground, I was relieved that my tent had not blown away and so I set to securing it. Then I hit the shower. I realized that I'd put my bra on inside out that morning. *Better inside out than backwards*, I thought.

I was considering driving back to Mt. Pleasant as the radio advertised a band festival in the evening. I was sweating too much to apply any makeup, and then I burned my forehead when I was trying to curl my hair, so I decided to stay at the campground and read. Also, I was still worried about my low tire.

At twilight, I lit a fire in the fire pit with my fire sticks and twigs that I had scavenged from the skirts of the forest. Then I returned to the scandalous lives of the characters between the covers of *Peyton Place*.

I still heard the sizzle and hiss of the embers when I zipped up my tent for the night. I pulled my quilt up to my chin and rested my cheek on my pillow. I was exhausted and content.

I thought about how my life was so different now, how good it felt to no longer be in an environment where I was unfairly judged. And I thought about how good it felt to finally be able to close my eyes at night without dreading the following day.

What I learned today: Hiking trails should have bus stops.

Day 6

I awoke at the first light of morning and decided to hop back on the trail in the park before I hit the road for my next destination. I liked this trial so much and it would get this old heart of mine pumping.

After an hour of hiking, I walked into the restroom and found the three sinks covered with dead bugs. Disgusting.

After my shower, a young mother walked into the restroom with a baby in a stroller. The baby had a perfect round face and perfect blue eyes. The girl looked just like the young actress from *Gilmore Girls*, very pretty. I recognized her as being part of the group that was camped in the condo-tent at the end of the road where I was set up. She told me a raccoon had jumped onto their picnic table the night before and took some hamburger buns when they were all sitting around the fire. It was a little scary, she said, as it was dark and all they could see were his menacing eyes.

I told her I was worried about my low tire, which had gone down overnight, and she said that Middleton had a Casey's General Store with an air hose.

I had visions of my tire going flat on the drive to Middleton. *What's the worst thing that could happen?* I thought. *If I get a flat tire, I'll just call AAA.* I repeated this over and over and tried not to notice the bright orange idiot light on the dash that mocked me.

I had to stop for a train to pass on the drive to Middleton. This took me back to my 3rd Grade class in Monroe. Train tracks ran behind the school and whenever a train passed, our teacher would stop our lesson and let us count the cars. This was a fun disruption.

My brow was soaked with worried sweat when I finally reached the Casey's Store. I filled my tire with air again and prayed I could make it to my next campground without incident.

I decided I would treat myself to an afternoon of browsing in a bookstore to distract me from my tire issue. I knew that Marion had a Half Price Bookstore and it was on the way to Central City, my next stop. I had to stock up for the next several weeks, after all.

After I'd filled up my book basket with bargain treasures, I pulled onto Highway 151. There was a Tires Plus that was open right in front of me. What luck! I thought I would have to wait until Monday to deal with my tire issue.

I pulled in and a friendly gentleman immediately came out and looked at my tire. He was quick to spot a nail. Why didn't I think to look? But what could I have done anyway? He said to give them 45 minutes to patch it up.

I guessed it had only been about 30 minutes when the gentleman called me and showed me the two-inch nail they had pulled from my tire. $32.09. Done. Now I could get on with enjoying my adventure.

It was 2:00 and 90-degrees when I got back on the road. I was feeling the heat, and so were the farm animals. Sheep were huddled like cotton balls under shade trees as I passed their grassy pastures.

I pulled into Pinicon Ridge Campgrounds about an hour later and found the perfect isolated spot surrounded by trees to pitch my tent. My own slice of heaven. There was just one other tent set up and it was down by the river. The fee was $15.00 a night here, not $11.00 since it wasn't a state park. I paid for four nights. I didn't care. This was a beautiful park and they offered plenty of hiking trails.

The Flying Squirrel Trail was right across the road from where I had pitched my tent, so I decided to check it out. It was a narrow dirt path, very steep and overgrown. I grew bored after a short time and turned around. I decided I would try another trail on the morrow.

I showered and then got into my jeep to drive around to the park entrance. What a clean, pretty park. I pulled out my lawn chair, found a big shady oak tree next to the river, and just sat and read a book for a while. My reading was interrupted by the lilt of birdsong, the croak of bullfrogs, and the plop of fish leaping out of the water every now and then.

When I returned to my campsite, I decided it was too hot and muggy for a fire. A cloud of gnats just wouldn't leave me alone. I wished I'd bought the tent with the screen porch. Finally, at 8:00, I crawled inside my tent to escape these annoying pests and read for an hour before falling asleep.

Whoosh! What was that? Something undeniably *big* had just rushed past my tent. Probably a deer. Or Bigfoot? It felt so close I could almost feel its steamy breath. But as long as it didn't rush *into* my tent, I was okay.

What I learned today: Nail goes into tire. Tire loses air.

Day 7

When Daniel Boone was asked if he had ever been lost, he replied, "No, but I was bewildered once for a few days."

The White Oak Trail was the trail from hell.

I drove past the boat ramp in the park, parked in the designated lot for the hike, and started to climb the trail. Or what I thought was the trail. Whatever path I was on ended abruptly after about a half-mile incline. I rechecked my map. Then I retraced my steps back to the parking lot, where I spotted a sign with an arrow that indicated the trailhead for the White Oak Trail was up the paved road.

After walking a short distance, I still couldn't find my loyal brown hiker man sign, so I got back into my jeep and drove up the hill, all the way to the group camping area and back down the hill. Finally, I noticed a small clearing with a grassy path on the right side of the road. Could this be it?

I decided to take my chances and give this path a try. I parked again and walked up the paved road to the clearing and turned onto the path. With fingers crossed, I forged ahead. I came across a wooden sign before long, so I knew I was on some sort of trail.

I skipped along, enjoying the tangle of the woods and the music of nature. The dirt trail led me up and down over heavily wooded hills and valleys. My skipping eventually turned to trudging. I had been on the trail for a very long time. I started to worry about finding my way out of the forest. I came to three intersecting paths. The posted sign didn't match my map. I began to panic. I had a feeling deep in my gut that I would never see my loved ones again.

I started down one path. It didn't feel right. I retraced my steps and looked at the sign and my map again. I tried another trail. This one didn't seem any more familiar, but I crossed my fingers and hoped it would lead me to the road. It just didn't feel like I was heading in the right direction.

I kept telling myself that it was early in the day, that I had no reason to panic, that I would eventually find my way out, that everything would be okay.

After what seemed like hours, the woods spit me out and into a picnic area. A deer was grazing nearby. He looked up at me for a moment, then went back to his lunch. I had no idea where I was.

I finally got my bearings and figured out that I was at the far end of the group campground area of the park. I had driven this road when I'd been trying to find the trailhead for this damned hike. I had a hell of a walk back to the parking lot. Snow would be falling by the time I reached my jeep. But there was no way I was going back into the woods.

I started walking.

The road was mostly uphill, and the sun was beating down on me ferociously. I cursed the opening to the trailhead as I passed it.

Just think of a cold beer, I thought, motivating myself. *A cold beer. A cold beer.*

After what seemed like two miles, my jeep was in sight. I hobbled to it like it was a mirage in a dessert. I felt it's hot surface. It was real. I had made it back alive.

A cold beer.

After I had regained my senses and sanity, I headed back to my campsite. I showered but didn't dry my hair. It was just too dang hot. (Do people normally bring hair dryers camping? I hadn't seen anyone else dry their hair.) I tossed on a straw hat to cover my unruly curls and pulled on a light cotton dress. I jumped into my jeep and made a quick trip to the convenience store along the highway. I needed nourishment.

I drooled over the four-pack of fresh cinnamon rolls with cream cheese frosting at the bakery counter. My weakness. That and cowboys. I resisted the temptation and bought a Chocolate Chip Fiber 1 bar and a block of hot pepper cheese to go with the Nut Thin crackers back at camp.

I decided I was going to get out my chair, go to the other side of the park like I did the day before, find a nice shady oak tree, and sit under it and read and drink. I deserved it after the bewildering morning that I had.

The gnats and flies attacked me as I built a fire in the fire pit in the early evening. I generously sprayed myself with insect repellent, especially around the face and neck, areas that they seemed to find particularly attractive about me.

The wind had picked up and the western sky was churning into a bruising purple. Would I experience my first camping storm tonight? Would I be scared in my tent? Would I be a fraidy-cat and run to my jeep?

What I learned today: There is a big difference between hiking two miles in the shady woods and walking two miles on hot pavement in the scorching sun. There just is.

~ ~ ~

I knew I had my facts straight. Yet, the Marketing Manager (let's call him Robert) refused to trust my knowledge during staff meetings. Instead, he would have a male non-manager verify my information. It was humiliating and degrading. I was, however, always proven right.

Robert, a suspender-clad Hispanic who liked exotic foods, regulary lunched with his male managers, the "good old boys". I always wondered what business conversations took place during these lunches that I was not privy to.

I remember that he included me only once in the lunch party. Robert drove us to a tiny Korean restaurant in a questionable section of town. I couldn't pronounce most of the items on the menu and I never eat anything that I can't pronounce. I finally found something that my mundane palate could stomach, fried rice, while Robert ordered squishy items that made me want to gag.

Considering his discriminitory treatment, I shouldn't have been surprised when Robert did not select me as one of his managers when we went through a reorganization. He did select one of his "boys", an employee who was not currently a manager in the department, as

I was. This employee also did not have a college education, as I did. I was put out to pasture, assigned to a postmaster position in a small office 40 miles from Des Moines.

But I didn't go without a fight. I filed a sexual discrimination case and it was settled out of court. As part of the settlement, I eventually got a manager's positon back in the Marketing Department after Robert had moved on.

Day 8

"Is this Heaven? No, it's Iowa."

I couldn't believe that I had never been to the Field of Dreams. I was so happy (and surprised) to see that this movie set was still such a tourist attraction.

It hadn't rained during the night after all, and today was expected to be another scorcher with the high reaching 94-degrees. I took off for Dyersville early, as it was probably an hour and a half drive, and of course, I missed the simple sign just north of town that pointed to the movie sight. I ended up in New Vienna and had to turn around and drive back.

When I pulled into the parking lot, it was mid-morning and the lot was almost full. There were quite a few people on the field taking pictures, and small children were running around the bases. I smiled as a little boy clumsily held a bat bigger than he was as his dad snapped a photo of him crouched over home plate.

I loved this movie when it came out in 1989, partly because I loved Kevin Costner. I had no desire to pay money to take a tour of the house, so I just browsed the souvenir stand for a while. They sold the usual mementos: t-shirts, key rings, postcards.

The visit to the site made me want to watch the movie again. And eat a hot dog.

I drove back to the campground and set off on the paved trail that linked the park to Central City. It was a beautiful walk. I saw many of my favorite feathered friends, including cardinals, bluebirds, and an oriole, along the way.

I was listening to the radio while I walked, and the station that I was listening to included an obituary segment. It reported that a 79-year-old man had been killed the day before when his tractor tipped over on him has he was going uphill in his field. How awful! Something similar happened to our neighbor when we were young. Dick had a heart attack while on his tractor, and fell off, and the tractor ran over him. I remember him as a man who was always smiling. I also remember that he would rub his scratchy whiskers against my young, fresh cheeks when he would give me a hug. Although miles separated our farms in Fairmont, we were as close as next-door neighbors.

After I'd gotten back to camp and showered, I caught my reflection in the mirror. Then I screamed. (Normally I just roll my eyes and sigh.) My forehead had two red burns on it from my curling iron, my nose was bright red from sunburn, my upper lip was swollen twice its size – a reaction I guessed from the insect repellent that I had sprayed on my face the night before, and my right eye was bloodshot.

I needed no whistle. My looks alone would keep all predators at bay.

I took my supper to the serene park area again and feasted at a picnic table along the river. A took off my straw hat and let the gentle early evening breeze dry my damp hair.

I then settled my chair onto a shady spot sprinkled with white clover. A bumblebee landed on a clover flower, sucked its sweetness, and then lazily buzzed onto another. This was how I had lived my adventure so far, just moving along at my own pace, drawing the wonder from one place before moving on. I smiled at the simple thrill of it all.

What I learned today: It's important to read the label warnings on cans of insect repellent. If it says not to spray on face, it is best not to spray on face.

Day 9

I unzipped my tent and a sharp breeze turned my attention to the dark sky and menacing clouds in the west. It was surely going to rain soon.

I decided it would be a good morning to spend at the laundromat. The gas smell from the waterproofer in my jeep had dissipated, but it had been replaced by an even more pungent odor: sweaty socks.

An elderly gentleman was sitting by the laundromat door and greeted me with a big smile when I entered. We made friendly small talk and then went about pretending to be interested in whatever was blaring on the television overhead.

I loaded a washing machine and slid into an uncomfortable plastic table and chair. A young frizzy-haired woman was staring at me. I caught her eye. This normally makes people glance away, embarrassed to be caught staring. Not this cheeky broad. I wanted to say, "Didn't your mother ever tell you that it was rude to stare?"

Then I remembered the condition of my face.

The threat of rain still thwarted any immediate hiking plans when I returned to my jeep with a load of freshly laundered clothes. *What a great day to get a little bit of education*, I thought, so I found myself on the road to Anamosa and the Grant Wood Art Gallery. "Granted", my knowledge of this artist was limited. Actually, I knew nothing about him, but I knew I was on the "Grant Wood" byway, according to the road signs as I drove through the scenic area.

The drive to Anamosa was spectacular. It was an uncontaminated landscape, a rich canvass of radiant greens and golds. Tractors kicked up dust clouds in the fertile fields. Cattle bunched together in their pastures and skittish goats pranced around barnyards with their choppy tails standing at attention. I left my windows down so I could let my lungs fill with the perfume of fresh country air.

The gallery didn't open until 1:00 so I had time to do a little browsing and shopping in town. I stopped into a "junk" store called, "Pistol Annie's and Coralbelle's Tea Room". The owner, a vibrant gal dressed in comfy jeans and a t-shirt, greeted me right away. I told her it was my first time in the lovely town of Anamosa, to which she said, "What, are you lost?"

She promoted her tea room located in the back, said that she had pies for sale, and asked if I would like a nice slice of blueberry pie. I declined. She told me quite assuredly that pies were "in" now and cupcakes were "out." Good to know.

We chatted away about anything and everything and when I left the shop I felt like I had made a new best friend.

I waited until 2:00 for the gallery to open, but it never did. I peeked inside the glass door and yearned to look around. There were prints (of course) and books and notecards and all sorts of other fun stuff like puzzles and magnets. The sky was clearing, so I decided to head back to the campground and get some exercise. I could always return. After all, I had all the time in the world.

I walked the length of the park trail into town again and thoroughly enjoyed the sounds of nature all around me before taking a quick shower. The cotton dress and straw hat were becoming my go-to outfit in this prickly heat.

I made a trip to the convenience store to buy more firewood and ice, and, what the heck...I was going to treat myself. I bought a 25-ounce can of Strawberita. That would be refreshing on this hot, humid night.

I loved the seclusion of my campsite. There was another camper down by the river, but I was alone in my special world. A beautiful kind of loneliness surrounded me as I watched the bright flames leap and the fireflies blink. I could hear the faint mournful sound of a train whistle in the distance. I took another sip of my Strawberita and picked up my book. I couldn't ask for anything more tonight.

Well, maybe a companion.

To get up and poke the fire every now and then.

What I learned today: Camping: Where I can look ugly and enjoy it.

Day 10

I woke to what sounded like a mini weed-whacker just outside my tent. What the heck? What insect could that be? And would it gnaw through the nylon fabric and eat me?

When I could no longer hear its annoying buzz, I unzipped my tent and went through the process of dismantling it. It was time to move on.

I showered and as I dried my hair, I felt something crawl across my toes on my right foot. I looked down and saw the biggest ant that I have ever seen in my life. I could put a saddle on this bug and charge kiddies for rides.

Palisades-Kepler State Park in Mt. Vernon was my next destination. I drove around the campground to check it out prior to paying, as I had started to do, in case I didn't like the park.

The first tent area had a non-reserved tent site available, which was next to a screened tent that was already set up. There was a shirtless man sporting a classic beer belly sitting inside sipping on a can of Budweiser. It was only 10:15 a.m. But who was I to judge?

Nope. This wasn't the site for me.

I drove around and discovered another loop just for tents. It was empty. I chose a prime spot and set up camp. Perfect. I registered and then drove off in search of the Cedar Cliff Trail inside the park. I struggled to find the trailhead and finally resorted to reading the directions in the guidebook. It was just off the beach area, past the parking lot.

The trail was a tangled scramble through the woods with frequent spots overlooking the river. I was amazed that I had lived in Iowa for so many years and had never known about all these beautiful parks and hiking trails.

Thank goodness there were wooden benches set up along the path, as I was huffing and puffing. I lifted myself onto one of them and felt like Lily Tomlin's Edith Ann character with my legs sticking out in front of me.

And that's the truth. Pffft.

What a wonderful feeling it was to be hidden in a forest surrounded by the exhilaration of nature. I could hear the tree branches and gentle breeze carry on a hushed conversation with each other. My heart was full.

I finally left the embrace of the woods and made my way back to my jeep.

The beach had filled with sun lovers and fishermen. A man was boiling in the sand like a Maine lobster. A woman was sitting in a lawn chair, her fishing pole securely planted in the sand next to her and a cigarette dangling from her lips.

It was late afternoon by the time I returned to camp. I showered and started in early on the liquid refreshments. I had really worked up a thirst from the tiring hike.

The shifting clouds in the western sky looked moody and menacing. I heard a low growling. Then I realized that I was hungry and reached for my box of crackers.

What I learned today: I like hanging out with me. I invite myself for beers at 4:00 in the afternoon.

~ ~ ~

Another postal reorganization loomed, and I was impacted once again. I had just returned from a week of hiking in New England and had loved it. On a whim, I applied for postmaster positions out east. I certainly didn't expect to get an interview, let alone to be offered a job.

My ex-boyfriend/still a good friend/more in his eyes said he would buy me a Z3 sports car if I would turn down the offer.

I packed my bags.

Stupid. Stupid. Stupid.

Shortly after I arrived in New Hampshire, the District Office discovered that I had a marketing background. As it turned out, the position that I had held in Des Moines was open in Manchester. They wanted me.

The District Manager (let's call him Mr. Bob), became my mentor and nominated me to participate in the Advanced Leadership Program. This was Headquarters' elite training program for the best of the best in the Postal Service. It was a top honor to be nominated, and graduation from this program guaranteed a paved future in the organization.

I was also placed on the register of the top employees in the Northeast Area, another honor. I was soon offered a high-level temporary assignment as Marketing Manager in Portland, ME.

During this time in Portland, I gave a Quarterly Review presentation to the Area Management Team from Boston, including the Area Vice-President, Megan Brennan. Afterward, the Area Marketing Manager came into my office and said, "Nice job! Megan was impressed with you!"

Had I known then that Megan Brennan was to become the Postmaster General of the United States just a few years later, I would have felt even more confident of my abilities.

I couldn't have been happier with the direction my career had taken. I was on top of the world.

Day 11

*F*irst, a few scattered raindrops tapped on the top of my tent. Then a distant rumbling followed by a quick flash against the darkness of the night. I pushed my cot into the middle of the tent. I had my flip-flips and my cute little teal flashlight ready in case I would have to abandon my tent and run for safety. This would be my first storm. I was excited. I was scared. Would I get soaked? Would the tent stakes hold? I snuggled deep into my sleeping bag and got out my rosary beads.

The wind whooshed, and my tent billowed. Another bright lightning flash followed by a thunderous clap. The storm was moving closer. The rain pelted against all sides of my tent.

The storm carried on and on. I counted the seconds between the lightning flashes and the thunder rumbles. The rain eventually lessened to just a few drops on my tent like the last kernels popping in a microwave popcorn bag. I had survived my first storm in a tent. And I would never forget it.

My last recollection of visiting the Amana Colonies was on a motorcycle with a small group of pals. It must have been 30 years ago. We went for the food. And we got what we went for.

I remember the bunch of us sitting around a family-size table and passing around large bowls of corn, mashed potatoes, gravy, all the fixings, just like it was Thanksgiving dinner. After filling our bellies, we staggered to a park and rolled onto the grass, too bloated to get back onto the cycles for the long drive home.

Ah, good times.

My visit to the Colonies this time was not for the food. I was interested in the Kolonieweg Recreational Trail that led around the lake in Amana.

I got on the paved trail at the Amana Depot, but it was uneventful, and I was quickly becoming bored. Eventually, it changed to a dirt path that led along the lake.

I soon caught up with a tall, lanky elderly gentleman wearing a long-sleeved pale, yellow shirt and baggy blue shorts that fell just above his boney knees. His face was lined with kindness and a beige floppy hat shielded his stark blue eyes.

"Some storm we had last night, huh?" I greeted him with small talk.

"We had a storm? I slept through it. I guess I was really tired from biking 40 miles," he said. "Or maybe it was the big supper that I had, with three pieces of blueberry pie for desert."

"You ate three pieces of pie?" I smiled.

"I was hungry after biking 40 miles." His grin showed crowded teeth that were yellowed with age.

I shared my hiking trip around Iowa with him and he talked about his favorite hiking trails in the country. Our conversation turned to travel in general and I was amazed at the places he had been. His eyes took on a kind of wistfulness when he spoke of Africa. He said that his fascination wasn't with the exotic animals themselves, but with their sounds. That was what he remembered most.

I loved talking to this interesting man. Soon he said it was time that he turned around, and he wished me a good trip. I was sad as I watched him walk away.

I continued walking until the trail led through a residential area. Dull. And it was getting hot. I wished I had the gentleman's floppy hat to shield the blazing sun from my face. I turned around and decided to head back up to Anamosa and the Grant Wood Art Gallery.

After stopping by my campsite for a quick shower, I was on my way.

Jo was knitting at a tiny wooden desk when I opened the door to the gallery. She greeted me with a warm smile that made me wish she was my grandmother. After I browsed for a few minutes, she asked if I would be interested in a short tour. Oh, my yes!

After spending an hour with this delightful volunteer, I didn't need to buy a book about Grant Wood. She had shared so much of her knowledge of this great artist with me.

When I left the gallery, I decided to head across town to the cemetery where Grant Wood was buried. I drove through the gray stones and carved tablets searching for his grave. At one point, I drove up along a single lane dirt path that had a precipitous drop. I was terrified that I was going to plummet over this narrow ledge and meet my maker. At least I would be in the right place.

One of Grant Wood's famous paintings was "Stone City" and it was well known that he caught much inspiration from this small town and the countryside that surrounded it. I had heard so much about the General Store Restaurant in Stone City, just a few miles from Anamosa, that I decided to make the trip and grab a bite to eat. And a cold beer.

The General Store was a stone two-story building set on the river. I opted to sit inside because it was so darned *hot* and all the tables on the deck were for large parties.

The friendly waitress suggested the Wapsi Wontons. Top these off with frosty beers and I was in Grant Wood Heaven. I sat there for some time and enjoyed the ambiance of the place. I couldn't determine whether I had a wobbly bar stool or if I'd just had one too many beers.

What I learned today: Nothing compares to experiencing my first thunderstorm inside a tent.

Day 12

*L*avender slippers. The owner of these had been in the toilet stall since before I took my shower. What could she possibly be doing in the toilet for so long?

A young girl, about ten, came into the restroom and I asked her if the storm had scared her the night before.

"No," she said, "I wasn't afraid, but my siblings were."

A woman came out of one of the showers and I asked her about the storm too.

"I didn't hear it, but I'm deaf in one ear, and I slept on the other," she said with a smile.

We struck up an easy conversation and learned so much about each other in just ten minutes. Kathy and her husband lived in Wisconsin, but they were here meeting their son. They were all camping together. She was a University of Iowa graduate and she impressed me with her education background, degrees I couldn't even pronounce. I told how I was a beginner at camping and that I was out hiking around Iowa and rediscovering the state I had missed so much.

She said that every time she returns to Iowa, she tells her husband, "Iowa just makes me feel good." Aw.

I could have chatted with Kathy all day. I bet she was a great best friend to some lucky girls in high school and college.

I left Kathy and the lavender slipper lady in the restroom/stall respectively and headed to the farmers market in Cedar Rapids.

I was lucky to get a parking spot just a block away from the market where there were tents of vendors selling fresh produce, flower bouquets, and handmade jewelry. Local wineries and breweries offered free samples. Street musicians were busking on every corner with their guitar cases open for tips. Market-goers filled their stomachs with warm breakfast burritos, egg sandwiches, mini-donuts, and other tantalizing treats. It was an early morning block party.

I picked out an adorable mini purse decorated with the Chicago Cubs logo for my sister from an elderly woman. I hadn't located an ATM yet, so the woman said she would take a personal check. I paid and thanked her and was already around the corner when I heard someone call my name. I turned around and the purse woman was chasing me.

"Maureen, you walk really fast," she said, a little out of breath.

"Here, I forgot to give you a free two-year pocket calendar." She handed me the small calendar and beamed. I thanked her and put the calendar in my purse. I smiled as I watched this kind lady walk away.

I browsed the market in unhurried delight, immersed in the fair-like feel to this event.

I was stopped by a friendly grey-haired man a little later. "So, what's your loyalty?" he asked. "You're wearing a Drake University t-shirt and Iowa flip-flops."

Before I could respond, he winked at me and walked away.

I passed on all the tempting treats at the market, but I did purchase several unique jewelry items. I returned to my jeep and decided to go to the Grant Wood Studio and Visitor Center since it was just a few blocks away.

There weren't any cars in the parking lot when I got there, and I wondered if the place was even open. I went up to the door and tugged on it. It stuck. Through the window, I could see two men in the darkened room and one stood up to let me in. He apologized for the sticky door. The other young man immediately put a tape about Grant Wood into the television, and I watched this with great interest, even though it mostly reviewed what I had learned from Jo the day before. I had become obsessed with this artist and his work.

At the end of the ten-minute tape, the docent asked if I would like to see the loft where Grant Wood lived for a time and painted some of his most famous works. Heck, yes!

We went outside to the side of the building and climbed the metal stairs. The docent had a clipboard in his hands with black and white photographs of how things looked when Grant Wood lived there before some changes had been made.

When I walked into the loft, I got this eerie feeling - the same feeling I had when I toured Graceland or saw one of Abraham Lincoln's stove pipe hats at Robert Lincoln's home in Hildene, Vermont. I was transfixed.

Since this was turning into a Grant Wood kind of weekend, I left the Studio and Visitor Center and drove to the Cedar Rapids Museum. I paid the $7.00 admission fee to just to see the Grant Wood exhibit. I think this was my first-ever visit to a museum. I'm just not a museum type of gal. I can't explain why.

I'd absorbed more culture in the past two days than I had in the past two decades. And I loved it.

Back to camp. The tent loop had filled up by now, and there was a party going on at the end. I had two male neighbors in the tents next to me with a couple of pre-teen girls. They were part of the party crowd. It might be a loud night. I wished I had earplugs.

It was still early enough for a good hike, so I searched out the other trail in the park. It was a short trail, but it really got my heart pumping: steep climbs, up and down, through the forest. I wanted more, but it was getting hotter. And I was hungry.

I took a sticky shower and then went back to the beach area to get away from the party bunch. It was pretty and relaxing here. My book was interesting, and my beer was refreshing.

I gazed at the soft yellow and orange hues of the early evening sky and thought about how much my life had changed in fourteen short months. When was the last time that I enjoyed a sunset? Now, a sense of deep contentment encircled me. I felt drunk with happiness.

What I learned today: A little culture is good for the soul.

Day 13

On November 17th, 1973, three Fryer brothers gunned down and killed four male teenagers and raped the thirteen-year-old female in the party. The young group was camping at Gitchie Manitou State Preserve in northern Iowa.

The Fryer boys were in the area poaching deer. They were spying on the innocent group of teens from afar and saw that they were smoking marijuana. They came up with a plan. They staged an impromptu police impersonation stunt to steal the marijuana, but the plan went bad. The brothers are serving life sentences.

I could hear the muffled sound of voices. I couldn't make out what they were saying. I checked the time on my iPhone. 2:37 a.m. The party at the end of the loop must have lasted a long time.

Two males were walking next to my tent. The road light threw their distorted silhouettes against my tent canvas. One of the males was wearing a cap turned backwards on his head. I felt sure that these two were working out a plan, a devious plan to rape and murder me. And steal my food.

I pulled out my watermelon tote bag from under my cot and fumbled around until I felt the cord of my whistle. I wrapped the whistle around my neck and crawled over toward the zipper closure of my tent to make sure the tiny padlock was secure. It was.

I dug around in my tote bag to see if I had anything else that would help me fend off these potential attackers. Deodorant. Nope. Book light. Nope. Curling iron. Maybe.

I grabbed my Iowa Hawkeye flip-flops, one in each hand, and thought I could pound the men with these rubber bad-boys.

I returned to my cot, rigid with fear, ready to face my fate. I wasn't going down without a fight.

I waited for them, expecting a knife to slash through the fabric of my tent at any moment. My whistle was in my mouth, as ready as a basketball referee watching for a foul. My flip-flops were positioned to do fatal injury if the situation demanded.

Hours later, I awoke curled on my cot with my whistle blocking one nostril and the flip-flops clutched to my chest like childhood dollies.

On my walk back from the shower, I saw these two men enjoying breakfast with their two daughters, acting just as innocent as could be. I shot them an evil eye as I passed their picnic table. They didn't look up.

It was time to move on. My next stop was Bellevue State Park, along the Mississippi River. When I pulled into the campground, I did a drive-through and checked out the restrooms and showers. The showers were separate from the restrooms, around the back of the building. Now that was different. I didn't think I was going to like going back and forth between the restroom and the shower. I registered for two nights instead of four, as I'd intended.

I quickly set up my tent, wiped the sweat from my face, and said to the older couple across the road from me, "At least there is a breeze today."

The gentleman said, "YES. THERE. IS." with such conviction that he almost knocked me into next week.

The first trail I wanted to hike started at the South Bluff Nature Center. The only other vehicle in the parking lot was a DNR pickup.

I passed a Garden Sanctuary for Butterflies shortly after beginning the hike. The trail had signs, but as usual, they didn't match my map, and they left me perplexed and puzzled. A scrawny, over-clad young man was walking some distance ahead of me. I noticed that he carried a clip-board and stopped periodically to scribble notes. I assumed that this guy belonged to the DNR truck and I was curious about his observations. I figured that if I followed him, I would eventually find my way back to my jeep.

The path gave way to a beautiful prairie. I felt like Laura Ingalls Wilder plodding home from school. The high grasses and wildflowers danced in the restless wind. I lost myself in the wonder of this place, this beauty. I closed my eyes and drank it all in.

I decided not to follow Mr. DNR any longer and turned around. I wanted to check out the other trail in the park while it was still early in the day and I still had the energy for it.

The directions to the trailhead in my guidebook were worthless. I wondered how much time I had wasted trying to find these over the past few days.

Finally, I found the hiker man sign and set off on the wooded trail. It was a long and exhausting trek and followed the river at one point. It ended abruptly at the highway, so I made my way back.

When I returned to camp, almost everyone had cleared out, including my neighbors across the road. I was glad, as the tent sites were close together and I like some elbow room. I gathered a bunch of twigs and set about building a fire.

My iPhone chimed and a text message from a former employee, Joanne, appeared on the screen. She asked about my adventure so far and said that staying in a tent alone was "gutsy".

Joanne and her husband had been camping regularly since she retired, but in a camper. I was always inspired by her story of the cross-country trip they'd taken in their VW van before they were married. They had made it as far as Wyoming before turning around and heading back to New England.

I would love to do that someday.

I will do that someday.

What I learned today: My brother-in-law was right when he said I should get a machete.

~ ~ ~

I could see the ghost of my first-grade teacher, Mrs. Hugan, nodding in agreement when the District Manager in Portland told me the reason she didn't hire me for the Marketing Manager position was that I wasn't assertive enough.

I returned to my job in New Hampshire after four months in Maine. Well, I returned to New Hampshire. Mr. Bob's "girlfriend" was in my job. And he wanted her to stay in my job.

When I met Mr. Bob in the hall shortly after I'd come back, he encouraged me to apply for the Portland position again, as it would be reposted. *Why would I do that?* I thought. *Why would I set myself up to get shot down again?* It was obvious that Mr. Bob did not want me back.

I had no job. They didn't know what to do with me. This was weird. Normally, whenever one returns from a detail assignment, they are slotted back into their job.

I wasn't included in the weekly Marketing meetings and was robbed of my previous responsibilities.

I just sat in a cubicle for eight long hours and pretended to look busy on my lap top computer.

Day 14

*S*eriously? I looked at the trail ahead of me and shook my head. How could I possibly climb this? Why would I possibly climb this? *I should be home putting together a jigsaw puzzle,* I thought.

My boots and my trek stick conspired against my rational mind and took off.

I was in the Mines of Spain State Recreation Center on a trail I wished I hadn't found. This trail, once I started it, did not level off, did not decline, did not do anything but expand my expletive vocabulary. Thank goodness it was a short trail. And I thought Iowa was supposed to be flat.

I found a much more tolerable trail, Horseshoe Bluff, which began as a mowed footpath. When I turned a corner early in the hike, I was shocked by the sight of a huge canyon with towering rock exposures. I was in awe. I couldn't believe I was in Iowa. This trail had signs at all junctions pointing to different levels. It was beautiful.

I just took my time on this trail and then drove around in the beautiful park before heading back to Bellevue mid-afternoon.

On the drive back on Highway 52, I felt as if I had stepped into a Grant Wood painting. The dramatic landscape and rolling hills were so breathtaking that I kept pulling over to snap photographs.

I saw a sign along the highway outside of St. Donatus that pointed to an "Outside Way of the Cross". I thought this sounded interesting, so I turned off. The signs led me to the town's catholic church, which was an imposing structure perched on a hill, overlooking the small town.

I parked in front of the church and walked toward the back, passing the ancient cemetery. Many of the tall gray tombstone's inscriptions were blotched by lichen but I could see that some of the leaning stones dated back as far as the 1880s. As I turned around, the sweeping view of the countryside was the most magnificent I had seen so far into this trip.

There was a gate on a slope behind the church that indicated "Way of the Cross and Pieta Chapel". I slipped through the gate with no idea of what was ahead of me.

Spread out at intervals up a long, winding hill were 14 small brick alcoves, each containing an original lithograph detailing Christ's journey to His crucifixion. It was built in 1861 and is believed to be the first of its kind here in the United States.

The outdoor Way of the Cross was built under the direction of Fr. J. Michael Flamming, the pastor of St. Donatus. He was an immigrant from Koerich, Luxembourg.

As I hadn't known what I would be finding here, I had just worn my flip-flops and hadn't bothered to strap on my knee brace or bring along my trek stick. The path along the "Way" was long, rough, and sometimes quite steep. Cow pies were scattered abundantly along the trail.

I was glad that I was alone on this spiritual walk. I raised my eyes to my Mother and Father in heaven to thank them for the strong faith that they instilled in me. Growing up on the farm, we would gather on our knees together after supper each night and pray the rosary. I remember one night, there was a program on television that all five of us kids really wanted to watch, so we conspired that when it came our turn to recite our decade of the rosary, we would say it really fast so we would be done in time to see our show. Mother, of course, was on to us. At the end of the rosary, she simply stated, "Okay, kids, let's pray the rosary again, the right way this time." We missed our show.

At the end of the "Way" stood the Pieta Chapel which was built in 1885. This is listed on the National Register of Historic Places. What a beautiful old church overlooking the valley. I took my time enjoying the view and the peace that surrounded me. It was worth the clumsy climb.

I stopped in Bellevue on my way back to the camp-ground. This town could have been the setting for a Hallmark movie - it was that quaint. A paved walking trail began at the gazebo and weaved along the river, its flower boxes filled with purple petunias. There were plenty of benches set along this path, where grandpas and their grandkids sat licking double-scoop ice cream cones.

I sat on a bench and lingered a while, letting the breeze from the river cool the sweat from my brow. Then I ordered a double scoop chocolate ice cream cone and headed back to the campground.

What I learned today: Flip-flops are not suitable footwear for hiking, especially on a trail covered with cow pies.

Day 15

T he first time that I went ziplining was in New Hampshire, on the ZipRider on Wildcat Mountain. My friend Jenny was visiting from Iowa. I had suggested this thrill before her arrival and she said, "No can do - I'm afraid of heights." No problem, I told her, there are plenty of other fun things to do here.

Well, when we drove past the zipline, to my surprise (and hers), she told me to turn around - that she could do it. Jenny's face was as white as a sheet, but she buckled into the harness and glided down the short wire line.

I went ziplining again in Gunstock, NH. This was more thrilling, but it had breaks in the route. Just when you would just get your adrenaline going, you would be stalled by having to move to the next line.

Sky Tours Zipline in Dubuque runs over Union Park, an area with rich history. This property is now owned by the YMCA, but in the early 1900s, it was quite the entertainment park.

Union Park had a dance hall called The Pavilion, a bandstand, a children's playground, a bowling alley, a roller coaster, a Wonder Cave, and trolley tracks to connect with the town. The Mammoth Theater (the largest theater in Iowa) was built there in 1909. It contained 1500 opera-style seats, followed by benches, plus room for thousands more too see the show (for free) on the hill outside, as the back wall was open.

In 1919, a flood destroyed most of the buildings. The park was rebuilt, but efforts to rekindle interest were unsuccessful and all the buildings were eventually dismantled in 1934. The YMCA bought the land in 1946 to use it as a residence camp. The zipline was added in 2011.

Reservations were required for the zipline, so I called when I was on the south side of Dubuque. The gal who answered the phone said I could get in with the 11:00 group. I had about 20 minutes to get there and told her that I would "zip" right up. She got my pun, giggled and said, "Cute."

The family that I would be joining had ziplined before too, so there was no fear factor in our group. The two young guides went through their standard briefing and then showed us how to get into the harnesses.

The female guide spoke so fast throughout the trip from line to line that my ears couldn't keep up. She had the perfect personality for this job and entertained us by adding her own genuine humor to the tour.

She had us pick up an animal bean bag before we took off on one line, so we could aim and toss it in a big red bucket on the ground as we zipped across. I picked out a lucky green bear with a shamrock on its chest, which I thought would be a sure winner.

The mother and daughter went across but didn't hit the bucket with their stuffed animals. The father offered for me to go next.

"I need a few more minutes to plan my strategy," I said.

He flew across and missed. I didn't have any better luck, even with my lucky bear and keen planning.

Guide Shelby was the last across and she hit the bucket like she had been doing it all her life.

The next line was a dual line and Shelby made it into a challenge: a race. The two teen siblings backed up in the dirt and made a run for it before they hit the open air. Next came the parents. I'm sure there was some trash talking going on before they got to the end of the line. Finally, the race was on between young, spritely Shelby and decrepit, crumbling me.

"I let her win," I said to the group when I finally landed. "Besides, I wanted to enjoy the view."

We moved on. I asked Marty, the male guide along the route, if they ever had anyone chicken out along the way. He said no – and that in fact, a man with Parkinson's Disease had made it through to the seventh line recently and a 90-year-old woman went the distance.

I envied the job these young guides had – swinging through the trees all day.

Shelby asked, while checking my harness on the last line, if I had enjoyed myself. "Oh yes," I said. "I love ziplines. It's funny that I love ziplining, but I'm terrified of roller-coasters." She said she felt the same.

After our last line, as we all walked back to the parking lot, Marty confessed to me that this was his first day working the zipline. He hadn't wanted to say anything to us earlier, as he didn't want to make us nervous.

I smiled to myself. His confession reminded me of the story of one of the first dates that my dad took my mother on. Dad loved trains and airplanes. He had arranged for them to go on a plane ride over his farm. Mother was so nervous about flying, but when she saw the elderly pilot, she assumed he was experienced, and her nerves were quickly calmed.

After the flight, the pilot shook Dad's hand and thanked him. "This was my first solo flight," he said. "I just got my license."

The Dubuque zipline wasn't thrilling, but it was certainly fun. The guides made the experience entertaining while sharing the great history of the area with us. I was so glad I had made time for this excursion.

It was early afternoon when I drove back through Dubuque. I decided to check out the Fenelon Place Elevator. This is the world's shortest, steepest scenic railway. It was built in 1882 and is just 296 feet in length. This gem is also listed in the National Register of Historic Places.

I parked in a spot at the bottom of the elevator, got out of my jeep, and looked up. And up. Good golly if it wasn't steep. I didn't have a fear of heights, but this elevator might just have given me cause to develop such a phobia.

I got into one of the cars and followed the posted instructions. I pulled the cord, which would alert the operator to start the car that would pull me to the top.

The car started moving, slowing taking me up. And up.

At the top, a gentleman behind a ticket window greeted me with a genuine Midwestern smile. Put a sailor cap on this man and he could have passed as the Skipper on Gilligan's Island. He said that if I was going back down, he would need $3.00.

"Is that all?" I asked. "Just $3.00?"

"Yes, we haven't raised our prices again today," he said with a wink.

I wasn't ready to go back down yet. Dubuque is such a picturesque city along the Mississippi River. I stood for a while and looked at the beautiful Victorian houses and historic buildings.

When I passed through the turnstile to make my way back down, Skipper joked that it was the other car that had the air conditioning and stereo.

I decided to return to the Pinicon Ridge Campground, as it was my favorite so far. Even though it was more money than a state park campground, it was worth it. Plus, it would be somewhat of a central site for visiting Maquoketa Caves and Backbone State Park.

I pulled into the campground and was relieved to find that my secluded site was available.

At bedtime, I tucked my ratty quilt around me. The solitary cry of a cricket just outside my tent sang me to sleep.

What I learned today: Swinging through the trees is just as much fun as walking below the trees.

Day 16

I got an early start for Maquoketa Caves State Park. I had a map from my guidebook listing all the caves and what I could expect from each. The family that had ziplined with me had said they'd been to the Maquoketa Caves. They advised to bring a flashlight and old shoes.

I went through my normal hiking prep routine, adding my cute little clip-on flashlight to my Iowa cap. I was ready for some 'spelunking'.

The first cave that I came across was the Dancehall Cave. It was the biggest and most developed of all the sixteen caves. This was a really cool cave, as it was lit and you could walk upright on a concrete walkway through to the end.

A trail weaved through the park, and all the caves along it were marked. The signs indicated whether each required belly crawling. Between these signs and the descriptions provided in my book, I was happy just hiking the trail that connected the caves. No belly crawling for this girl.

When I'd had my fill of the caves (or the hike around the caves) and returned to the parking lot, it was full of parents with children who were anxious to crawl into dark places and get wet and muddy. Have at it, little ones.

I got on the road and headed to Backbone State Park.

I had been to Backbone State Park twice before. The first time was with my best girlfriend and her family when I was 13. We stayed in a cabin. I sent a postcard home and made a note to Mother, "I fell and broke my glasses. I'm okay." She kept this postcard and I found it among her things after she passed. Funny that I'm still clumsy.

My sister Sheila and I rented a cabin at Backbone when we were in our twenties. All I remember doing that week was watching television on the small portable black and white set that we'd brought along and stuffing our faces with junk food. It was a great week.

I followed the signs to the east entrance of the park and started walking, first on the popular Backbone Trail. This was a short winding path through the forest.

I passed a young, anxious woman who was stuck on top of a boulder like a kitty caught on a high tree branch. Her significant other was trying to coax her down from the perch and wasn't having any luck. Did I hear the sound of a fire engine?

The loop ended too soon. I noticed that the East Lake trailhead was just on the other side of the road. According to my book, it was a long trail, but I felt up for it.

I set off, thoroughly enjoying the rugged scenic path along the lake. I was in heaven. I came to a junction in the trail, which, according to my map, was about the halfway point. I so wanted to go the distance, but it was getting on in the afternoon. I had started to trip over my feet, an early sign that I was getting weary. I stood at the intersection for some time, the path ahead beckoning me.

Finally, I turned around and told myself that if I had time, I would return to complete the hike. I collected a fistful of twigs at the trailhead for a fire later and headed for the campground. It had been a good day of hiking and I was exhausted. I needed a hot shower and a cold beer.

After I showered, I slipped into my cool cotton dress and drove around to the picnic side of the park. I found a shady spot and feasted on crackers, cheese, and guacamole.

I had hoped for privacy to read, but a dusty SUV soon pulled up close to me and an elderly couple slowly got out and retrieved fishing gear from their hatchback. They unfolded chairs next to the river some distance apart from each other and tossed in their lines.

The man was wearing denim bib overall shorts with no shirt underneath revealing leathery tan skin. His sneakers were new white and his socks reached mid-calf. The woman wore dungarees rolled up to her knees, a printed blouse that a woman her age would wear, white anklet socks, and Keds tennis shoes.

They sat in silence. Soon, the old woman began to softly hum.

Fishing looked relaxing.

Fishing looked boring.

After an hour or so without a bite, the couple packed up their SUV and left the park.

I wondered if I should take up fishing. I wouldn't have the frustration of trying to find trailheads. But I was afraid of slimy fish and squishy worms.

Scratch that idea.

What I learned today: "Spelunking" is more fun to say than to do.

~ ~ ~

Mr. Bob was a bully. It was best not to get on his bad side. Which was exactly the risk I was taking when I called his friendly secretary to set up an appointment to see him.

I was nervous as hell when Christine said I could "go on in" after I'd been waiting for five minutes outside Mr. Bob's office. But I just couldn't take another day of being treated like I didn't exist.

Mr. Bob was wearing his usual red paisley-patterned suspenders and a starched white shirt. He shook my hand and motioned for me to sit in the stiff chair across from his mahogany desk which dominated the space in his office.

I respectfully thanked him for all the opportunities he had given me since my arrival in New Hampshire. I said that I felt like I didn't have the support from him that I once had. I needed to know what I had done and what I could do to fix it.

His rosacea cheeks turned purple. He shook his finger at me and pounded his fist on his desk. He made accusations that shocked me because they were so totally false and ludicrous. But in his rabid condition, I knew it would do no good to try to defend myself.

I sat perched in that damn stiff chair and took everything he threw at me.

When he'd finished, I returned to my cubicle, stunned by what had just happened. I knew then that my career in the New Hampshire District was over.

Day 17

*F*red Hoiberg. the head coach of the Chicago Bulls and former Iowa State University basketball coach, was working at the Pulpit Rock Campground.

Well, he sure looked like Fred Hoiberg. Blond. Tall. Cute. I told him I needed a tent site for the next three nights. He checked me in and looked out the window at the gloomy sky.

"Have you heard the forecast for the rest of the day?" he asked.

"Yep."

"At least you'll be able to set up your tent before it starts raining."

"I hope so."

I drove to my site which was alongside the river. It had already started to sprinkle, and so I grabbed my pink rain jacket from the back of my jeep. If nothing else, I was stylish.

I rushed to assemble my tent, and just then the wind picked up. I hadn't yet secured the tent to the ground with the stakes. I hugged it with both arms, desperate to keep it from tumbling into the river.

Once I was set up, I decided to wait out the brewing storm and do a little shopping in town. By the time I had filled my shopping bags and emptied my pocketbook, the skies had cleared. I was eager to check out the Trout Run Trail.

I parked at the Fish Hatchery. Shortly after I'd begun my walk, I rounded a bend to find several people standing in the middle of the trail sporting cameras with huge lens attached that were aimed upwards. I discovered from brochures about local attractions that there was an eagle's nest in the high limbs and this was a popular place for eagle photographers. In fact, there was a webcam installed in the nest so that people worldwide could watch the eagles' family life.

I got a good walk in along this trail just before the clouds darkened and the sky opened up. What to do now? What about a drive? Okay.

The World's Smallest Church, just south of Decorah, would be a nice jaunt.

The country drive to the small chapel in Festina was well marked. This tiny church was constructed in

1885 as the result of a vow by the mother of Johann Gaertner, a soldier in the French army who served under Napoleon. His mother vowed if her beloved son returned safely home from the Russian campaign, the church would be built in his honor. He survived and is buried on this site.

The church measures 14 x 20 feet and seats only eight people. So sweet.

What I learned today: It was doubtful that Fred Hoiberg needed a summer job working at a campground.

Day 18

*W*hat the heck was an effigy mound?

I had no idea, but I was about to find out. I was the only person in the National Park Service visitor center so early in the day. The friendly (and handsome) guide greeted me when I plucked a hiking brochure from the display on the wall. I cursed myself for not having read my book, "How to Make Anyone Fall in Love with You". He invited me to view a short video about the mounds and the history of the area.

I learned that effigy mounds are earthen sculptures shaped like birds, bison, turtles, and most commonly, bears. The mound builders inhabited the Upper Mississippi River Valley in Iowa, Illinois, Minnesota and much of Wisconsin between 750 and 1400 years ago. It is believed they sculpted these mounds as part of their religious ceremonies and burial traditions.

In 1949, President Harry S Truman declared Iowa's effigy mounds a national monument. They constitute an ancient burial ground and are considered sacred by many. Of the 191 known mounds within the site, 29 are shaped like animals. At 650 feet, the Great Bear Mound is the largest effigy mound that remains in Iowa.

I set off on the hike and was met immediately with a steep incline. The path was blanketed with wood mulch, which I found curious. But it was a good thing, as I'd been worried the path would be muddy after the heavy rain from the night before.

A gust of wind suddenly shook the branches of the trees above, causing the leaves to shudder. Rain streamed down on me, a peaceful shower under a bright blue sky. I spread out my arms and lifted my face to the wet sun. This was the kind of moment that just couldn't be expressed with words.

Before long, there was short detour off the trail which led to a majestic view of the Mississippi River. I shrugged off my backpack and settled onto the wooden bench. Looking out over the beautiful Mississippi, my thoughts drifted to my past, the costly decisions that I had made, and the gratitude that I now felt that I was back home where I belonged.

I have always been a firm believer that "everything happens for a reason", but I have never been able to figure out why God guided me to New Hampshire fifteen years ago. After I accepted the job transfer, I wanted to change my mind, but the District Manager had already announced my reassignment to all employees in Des Moines and I had made a commitment to my new boss in New Hampshire. I felt like it was too late. It wasn't all bad, moving to New England. I loved the mountains and the ocean. I made a few life-long friends. But, overall, it was fifteen years of my life that I wish I could do over. I never would have left Iowa.

I took my time on this trail, breathing in the tranquility, the solemnness of the place.

On my way back to the parking lot, the downward slope felt as challenging as the climb up had. I wished I could roll down the hill as I remembered doing for fun as a child. Or better yet, become a human Slinky.

The visitor center was busy when I returned around noon. The handsome employee advised that the wood chips were used for preservation of the trail.

What a workout I'd had today! Three miles of strenuous terrain plus two miles on the Trout Run Trail before I'd left Decorah. And I still wanted more. I checked my books for other hiking trails in the area.

I drove north of Decorah, passed the trailhead for Malanaphy Springs State Preserve and had to turn around. My book warned the sign would be small. Yep.

As I prepped for this hike, two SUVs pulled in across from my jeep and a group of eight or ten middle-aged women got out. They formed a huddle like a football team in the middle of the parking lot. They were all built like linebackers and frankly, I was a little afraid.

They grunted something incoherent and hit the trail. I let some time go by to create a little distance between this band of linesmen and me.

This beautiful one-mile walk led to a spring and waterfall. The dirt path took me up and down and I had to clamber over many fallen logs.

When I got to the waterfall, the group of women was attempting to climb the impossibly steep path up the side of the falls. I thought I would pass on this. I didn't have a death wish.

It was only 2:30 and I still had a lot of energy, but I had already hiked approximately 7 miles total today. I was hungry, and I smelled really bad - so bad that the mosquitos wouldn't even come near me. It was time to shower and get something to eat. And drink.

After I showered, I went to Phelps Park in town to dine instead of the campgrounds. It had filled up, and I had neighbors on both sides of me. I wanted a little privacy.

When I returned to my campsite, the neighbors to my right were cooking hot dogs and the neighbors to my left were trying to soothe their crying baby. Did people really bring newborns camping? I guessed so.

I built a fire, plugged in my MP3 player to block out the conversations and baby cries, and picked up my book. These sites were just too darn close together. It was too bad, because the riverside location was beautiful.

After my neighbors had got their fill of dogs, they took off for town to see a movie. Yay. I retired to my tent after my fire had turned to ashes and was just entering dreamland when these neighbors returned and decided to reignite their fire and have a midnight snack.

"One s'more or two?"

"One is the most I can do."

"Why?'

"I can never eat more than one s'more."

"I'm gonna have two. Maybe more since I have the fire going."

"Maybe I will try two."

All right already! I thought. *Eat your damn s'mores and go to sleep!*

What I learned today: Movie theaters should sell s'mores.

Day 19

I was glad I didn't give up on the Weeping Rock Trail at Pike's Peak State Park located near McGregor. I'd happened on it by accident and had just about turned around because it was so boring. It began as a mowed footpath and there was just nothing exciting about it on either side or in front of me. I'm always after a good stretch of the legs and this trail was 1.65 miles one-way, but I also needed some sort of scenery to keep me interested.

But I kept going, hoping that it would transform into something... anything.

And, by golly, it did.

The trail soon turned into the most wonderful walk through a wooded wonderland. At one point, I heard rustling on the hill above me. A curious deer stared down at me. When I turned to my right, I saw what this trail had been named after. Water was trickling down from layered rocks. It was breathtaking. I kept going and the trail kept getting prettier.

As I was reaching the final ¼ mile on my return, I approached a cute young couple. The gal noticed my leg brace. She said she had a bad knee too, from years as a cheerleader.

"Too many flips?" I teased her.

I didn't tell her how I had torn my meniscus. I twisted my knee when I was putting on stilettos to meet a girlfriend for a night out on the town.

"Do you know your leg is bleeding?" she asked, pointing to my left leg.

I looked down and saw a dried trickle of blood extending from mid-calf to my ankle. "Oh, that." Note to self: stop and buy another box of Band-Aids.

We chatted away as if we were old friends, and I told her that I dreaded the day when all I'd be able to do was hobble to the overlook and appreciate the view. By God, I was going to keep hiking just as long as I could.

As we parted, I told her that I expected her to cartwheel down the path. She and her boyfriend laughed and continued on their way.

I still had a lot of energy after the long drive back to Decorah, so I decided to return to the Trout Run Trail. But first, I needed more food. I stopped in the local market and grabbed chips with a touch of lime and a can of bean dip. The sky had become gray and sullen and the rain let loose when I exited the store. I made a mad dash to my jeep and munched on my snack behind the steering wheel.

The dip sounded better than it tasted. I dunked just a few chips in the disgusting -looking mess and decided to toss them both.

I looked up at the sky, wondered if the rain would let up and whether I could get a hike in. I peered through the blurry windshield and saw a Goodwill Store before me! Holy cow! My senses must have been failing me. Normally I can sniff out those stores a mile away.

Heck with the hike. A treasure hunt was in store for me.

I left the store with a box full of bargains. Four books at $1.00 each, an Old Navy fleece pullover for $2.50, a tin Green Bay Packers bank in the shape of a football for my sister for $3.00, and a small backpack for $1.49. I had scored big-time.

I never shop at shopping malls. I couldn't even remember the last time I had been in a mall. I hate them. I buy all my clothes at Goodwill. Except for my underwear. That would be creepy.

My shopping spree was finished and so was the storm. I got in a nice walk and then returned to the crowded campground. I noticed that I had new neighbors. The baby family was still there, but the girls on the right had left and a new tent was up.

I shut out the noises of the other campers and became entranced by the reckless flames of the fire. A gang of crickets chirped in the thickets. There was a soft glow drifting above the river, the blush of a dying day.

What I learned today: Tent sites are too close together when you can hear your neighbors snoring.

~ ~ ~

Late in the afternoon after the disastrous meeting with Mr. Bob, I was called to my direct manager's office (let's call her Ms. Bobette). I tapped on her open door. She quickly hid a jumbo bag of animal crackers in her desk drawer and instructed me to sit down in the chair across from her.

Then she presented me with a Performance Improvement Plan (PIP), the first step in the process of termination.

Ms. Bobette, of course, was Mr. Bob's puppet in this process. She was my direct boss, so he had to go through her to accomplish his goal – to fire me.

I asked a good friend of mine who'd also had his battles with Mr. Bob, why he had reacted the way he did during our meeting the previous day. My friend said that I had put Mr. Bob on the spot, and no one puts him on the spot.

I think it was more that he wanted to keep his girl-friend in my job.

Ms. Bobette, surely under the orders of Mr. Bob, had created the PIP in haste, obvious by its lack of merit.

One item on the PIP required that I call upon my counterpart in Boston to serve as a mentor to improve my organizational and planning skills for my role in the Postal Customer Council. She had already called her counterpart to set this up. This was humiliating.

I asked her if she had ever attended an event that I had organized.

"No."

I asked her if she had received negative feedback from the events that I had organized.

"No."

Then I asked her why she thought I needed training in this area, an area that I considered to be one of my strengths.

Her response, "Just a feeling."

Huh? I thought. *Excuse me? A feeling? You are going to use this PIP as a tool to terminate me based on a feeling?*

"Irregardless, Eileen will be calling you this week."

Her frequent use of the non-word "irregardlesss" irritated me like fingernails on a chalkboard.

"And your email messages! Why do you have to send me so many email messages?"

"What?" I blinked. "I had no idea that emails upset you. How would you prefer that I communicate with you? By phone? In person?"

"Anything," she drawled. "Anything but those damned emails!"

Wouldn't a good manager address this issue with her subordinate, so the behavior could be corrected before developing a plan for removal? I thought.

Early the next morning, Ms. Bobette entered my office and pushed the PIP and an ink pen under my nose insisting that I sign next to her signature. I was surprised that she was surprised when I refused to sign the document.

Mr. Bob evidently thought I was just a simple farm girl from Iowa. He didn't know that this farm girl had some fight in her.

I hired an attorney.

Day 20

The middle-aged woman looked at me over her cheater glasses and said, "The bogeyman might get you up there."

I smiled. "I'll be fine."

"There's no light up there, no electricity."

"I know."

"No outhouse."

I nodded.

"You've been here before?" she asked.

"No, but I just drove up there to check it out. Could I have site #12, please?"

"We do have a few tent sites by the river," she said. This woman was doing her best to talk me out of staying in the 'upper deck' tent site, the part of the campground that was located above the RV and camper area.

"Most tent campers prefer the river sites. The others are too secluded, too primitive."

"That's what I like about them," I said.

She removed her glasses and moved to the computer. "Okay," she said with a sigh. "Let's get you in here." She pulled up the campground map and did whatever she needed to do to get me into tent site #12.

"I'll need $20.00 for the night."

"Two nights, please."

She swiveled back around in her chair and punched a few keys on the key pad.

"$40.00"

"I also need a bundle of firewood," I added.

"That's another $5.00. You can just help yourself from the cart out front."

She ran my credit card through, gave me a smile of apprehension, and told me to enjoy my stay.

I drove through the campground and turned at the sign pointing to the upper tent sites, #9 – #14. The narrow dirt path was a steep incline that led me to a small, level area. I wondered if the track would even be passable after a good rain.

I set up my tent just a few feet from the forest line. How I wished that I could whistle – I was that happy. This site was paradise. Woods surrounded the area and I was sheltered by a canopy of trees. No one in the world knew where I was. And I liked it that way.

It was late afternoon and I decided to take a road trip to the northwestern most town in Iowa: New Albia. My map showed orange dots along County Road A26, indicating a scenic route.

"Scenic" was inadequate to describe this drive. The fading sun cast its light upon the rolling hills and serene countryside. I couldn't believe that such gentle grandeur existed in Iowa. I turned down Highway 26 and made my way toward Lansing where I caught glimpses of the Mississippi River through the thick expanse of trees.

I pulled off the highway to check out the Fish Farm Mounds State Preserve and Wildlife Area just north of Lansing. This area consisted of thirty middle-late woodland burial mounds that had been constructed between 1,350 and 2,100 years ago. I bounded up the short trail from the parking lot, but all I got for my efforts were blasted mosquito bites. If a trail existed in this preserve, I couldn't find it. I was disappointed, but I was getting used to disappointment by now.

I returned to the campground around 7:00 and couldn't believe how it had filled up. The small pond was still crowded with kids and adults alike. Campers and RVs were waiting in line to register. I could see why this was such a popular place.

I drove up to my campsite and was relieved to find that no other tents had joined me. I set about collecting twigs and it wasn't long before I had a crackling fire going in the pit. I noticed a beige toy soldier partially buried in the dirt around the fire pit. Was some little boy missing his toy?

I opened a cold beer, pulled out my current read, *My Antonia*, and settled into my chair. Long lazy shadows stretched across the grass. I heard the wind sigh and the trees yawn. Another day had come to a close.

The cicadas' singing competed with the voices and laughter that wafted up from the campers below. I caught a wink of a firefly. Then another. I closed my eyes and deeply inhaled the sweetness of the summer air.

I smiled and let the joy of being completely at peace spread over me.

"It is in the still silence of nature where one will find true bliss." Amen.

What I learned today: Life is good when the toughest decision of the day is "One beer or two tonight with supper?"

Day 21

When I hear, "Shoo!" I think of my mother hanging clothes on the line when we lived on the farm. She would shout, "Shoo!" at pesky chickens to get out of her way as they pecked around her feet.

I hiked all day on the beautiful trails at Yellow River State Forest. I had so looked forward to that part of my adventure and it didn't disappoint.

So, I was ready for another relaxing evening at the campground, what might be my favorite site yet. So secluded. So quiet.

I built a nice fire and watched the logs sizzle, pulsing orange embers almost hidden behind gray ash. Whispers of smoke swirled upward, and a light breeze carried them away.

A teenage boy drove up in an ATV to check the two large garbage cans at the curve of the road. He gave me a quick look and waved as he passed.

I noticed I'd been getting funny looks from other campers throughout my adventure. I wondered if was because:

   a. I was camping alone.

   b. I was a woman camping alone.

   c. I was an old woman camping alone.

The drowsy sun had given way to a mellow evening. Day and night were colliding. Again tonight, I could faintly hear the mingled voices from the campers below. I took the last swallow of my beer, pushed myself out of my chair, and walked the few feet to my jeep to put the empty bottle into a plastic bag with the rest of my trash.

I locked my jeep and gathered my book from the ground beside the chair where I'd left it. Then I unzipped my tent. It was time to turn in. I plopped down on my cot, book in hand, and attached my flexible book light to the back cover of the book.

A few minutes later, I could hear what sounded like fireworks going off. Fun! I unzipped my tent, stepped outside and looked to the dusky sky. I was disappointed that the canopy of trees from my hilltop campsite blocked any sort of view. I re-entered my tent and settled for just the sounds of the show – the booming and popping and hissing.

It wasn't long before the fireworks were over, and I was able to concentrate on my book. I sympathized with Mary Lincoln as she was about to be admitted into an insane asylum by her son, Robert.

I was at that place between dozing and consciousness, when suddenly an unknown critter bounded out of the woods and charged into the back of my tent. His body rammed mid-height into the tent and bounced off like it was a trampoline.

I jolted upright on my cot and shouted at the acrobatic creature, "**SHOO!**"

It made some sort of growly noise, but my knowledge of killer critters was limited (actually, non-existent), so I couldn't identify it by sound.

I knew it was too small to be a bear. A bear would have torn down the tent and eaten me alive. And I knew it was too big to be a raccoon. What was it?

I could hear this monster slowly circling my tent. I turned on my lantern and fumbled in my tote bag for my whistle.

Obviously, "Shoo" hadn't scared it off.

I knew that blowing my whistle wouldn't bring any help. I was too far above the campers. They would never hear me. But would it scare off this beast?

Each crunch of a twig sent another shiver of fear along my spine. Each passing minute seemed like an hour.

I waited. I listened.

Finally, all I could hear was the chattering of my teeth.

I grabbed my pillow, quilt, lantern, and the remote control to my jeep.

How far away had I parked? I had to make a run for it. Whatever the monster was, if it was still out there, could I outrun it? I thanked God that I had my sneakers in my tent instead of my flip-flops. That gave me hope.

I stood and gave my knees a few minutes to quit shaking. When I hit the remote -control button to unlock my jeep, it would also turn on the lights. That would surely frighten the beast, and if it was still out there, it might retreat into the woods.

Okay, on the count of three. One, two, three!

Click the remote, unzip the tent, zip the tent, *run!*

The ten feet between my tent and jeep seemed like the length of a football field. No wonder I never went out for track in high school.

I made it! I got the quilt caught in the door, but I was alive!

I locked the doors and scanned the campsite with the light of the headlights. No monster prowled about. My body trembled so violently that my jeep rocked.

I wondered if I would be able to stay another night in the woods, in a tent. Would I have to continue my hiking tour around Iowa by staying in hotels? I was only halfway through my adventure!

What I learned today: "Shoo!" is only effective for frightening away chickens or other barnyard pests.

Day 22

A hint of sunlight was flickering through the trees when I awoke at 6:00. I was surprised that I had slept at all. I thanked God that the monster hadn't attacked my jeep in the night, broken through the windshield, and devoured me.

I looked around the site and didn't see any creatures shrouding behind the trees, so I cautiously stepped out and spilled my stiff body onto the ground. I ignored the shooting pain in my hip and set about the process of taking my tent down. I was so glad to be leaving this campground and the unknown beast.

As I went to lift the hatchback of my jeep, I noticed defined paw prints in the dust of the rubber bumper. Could this be evidence of the critter that had stalked me the night before? Could I identify the beast from these prints? I took pictures to submit to the lab.

Mist lingered above the pond as I pulled out of the campground. All was quiet. I had completed my tour of eastern Iowa. And oh, how I had enjoyed the visit.

I needed a peaceful respite from the terror of the night, and the drive to the Hayden Prairie State Preserve just west of Cresco provided me with just that. I felt like I was thumbing through a picture book of Iowa as I made my way west. Cows lazily lifted their heads from their grazing as I drove past their pastures. Beams of sunlight shone on the pristine farmsteads as if they were stars on Broadway. My eyes swept across the wide expanse, seeing nothing but simple country loveliness. How could I have ever left this state?

I found the State Preserve with no problem (now that's something new), but there was no trail as I had hoped there'd be, and I didn't want to walk around the perimeter of the preserve on the county roads. So, Plan B.

I jumped on the Wapsi-Great Western Line bike trail for a nice long walk. I found one of the trailheads behind a park in Riceville and took a leisurely stroll. I was pleasantly surprised to come across a bird garden and stopped a while to watch my favorite birds enjoy lunch at the feeders.

After that, the moment of truth. I pulled into the Pilot Knob Campground and slowly weaved my jeep through the grounds. Could I muster the courage to stay in a tent again after the sheer horror of the night before?

I hemmed and hawed. Waffled. Shillyshallied. Vacillated. Dithered.

I circled the tent sites again and again, my courage building with each loop.

I found a site that still was a bit isolated, but I loved it.

Decision made!

I quickly set up camp and then took off for the Lime Creek Conservation Area just north of Mason City, an hour drive or so.

Yes, I'd died and gone to heaven. This place was paradise. There were several trail loops around the square prairie patches that were bursting with wildflowers. The paths were wide mowed grass making for an easy stroll. This was exactly what I needed, as the temperature was already above 90-degrees.

A gentle breeze accompanied me as I made my way around the loops. The aroma of freshly cut grass surrounded me, intoxicating me with its sweetness. Dragonflies and bumblebees mingled among the flowers and crickets cried in the tall grass.

I relaxed for a while on a bench and gazed at the wildflowers dancing in the wind. The joy in my heart that had been repressed for so many years was being released like a butterfly freed from its cocoon. I was beginning to live again.

I reluctantly returned to my jeep as the afternoon faded. The humid air had sucked the energy from me. I couldn't wait to get back to camp to wash the sticky sweat from my body.

After I'd showered, a tiny worm on the tile floor caught my attention. He crawled forward using his countless tiny legs. Then he crawled backwards using his countless tiny legs. Back and forth, he went nowhere. It reminded me of climbing up on a down escalator.

What I learned today: No measly critter is gonna keep me from continuing my adventure!

~ ~ ~

It got ugly.

Mr. Bob would not acknowledge me when we passed each other in the hall. That did not keep me from greeting him with a friendly 'hello' and a smile. This certainly infuriated him more. And he was our leader?

I had always felt that Ms. Bobette resented the fact that I graduated from the Advanced Leadership Program before she did. Now she deliberately showed her dislike for me. She blatantly excluded me from lunches with all her other managers. I was always the last to know about any changes in staff or company policies, if I was informed at all.

I was no longer second in command in the Marketing Department, even after holding the high-level Manager's position in Maine for a period of time. I had been replaced with a lower-level manager with much less experience and fewer qualifications. It was demeaning to have to take orders from a junior manager when Ms. Bobette was on leave.

I was being punished for unjustified reasons. The discrimination case I'd filed surely didn't help matters any.

But I continued to give my job everything I had. I arrived at work each morning before anyone else and was the last one to leave in the evening. I knew I had to keep up my performance.

But it was torture working for these wicked people.

I used up all my complimentary Employee Assistance Program counseling sessions and then sought weekly private therapy. My therapist suggested that I picture Mr. Bob and Ms. Bobette in a laughable situation when I got too depressed. I envisioned them as ogres (which wasn't much of a stretch) living under a bridge among stinky garbage with rats scuttling about their feet. And they were wearing soiled diapers. I liked this visual.

I swallowed anti-depressant and anxiety pills like they were jelly beans. All because this pair of managers was making me feel completely and utterly worthless.

I was broken.

Day 23

$\mathcal{M}$ other would turn over in her grave if she knew I had embarked on this adventure. When I lived in New Hampshire, she worried when I told her that I hiked the trails in the White Mountains alone. She was terrified that I would take a bad fall and tumble over a cliff. Mother never knew about the moose and bear that I met on my hikes. I thought it best not to share these particular details with her.

The hike in the Pilot Knob State Park looked like it would be challenging, based on my guide books, but I was well-rested and ready. I thought a nice scenic view would be an inspiring way to begin a day of hiking.

I took the short uphill gravel path from the parking lot that led to the Observation Tower. It was a round stone tower that is listed on the National Register of Historic Places. It also has one of the highest elevations in the state. I climbed the 48 metal steps inside and gawked at the view from the top. I was 1450 feet up.

Enough pleasure - I was ready to get my boots dirty and my hair messy.

I made my way back down the hill and crossed the parking lot to the trailhead. I was wearing capri stretchy pants to keep my legs dry. I thought the trail would be wet and muddy from the heavy rain the night before. It was.

It wasn't long before I came to a fork in the path. I was befuddled. I pulled out the map that I had tucked into my waistband and consulted it. There was no fork on the map at this point. I checked to make sure that I'd torn out the correct hike from my book. Was I even on the right trail? I was.

I heard voices. Not just the usual ones in my head, but real human voices. Three ladies appeared from the left path and greeted me. I showed them my map and explained my dilemma. They told me that the path they were on was the one I wanted. I would soon reach a bench that would lead me around the lake.

I thanked them and went happily on my way.

Not long after I passed the bench, I came to another multi-fork. I pulled out my map. No multi-fork on my map. Again, stymied. Then something occurred to me. *I should read the instructions.* So I did.

I followed the detailed directions, which took me around Dead Man's Lake. As I walked, my boot struck something on the ground, and it cartwheeled in front of me. At first, I thought it was just a rock or twig. I bent down to pick up a toy soldier identical to the one that I had found next to the fire pit at the campground that I'd just left. This seemed worthy of a wish or something. I put it in my backpack for luck.

Eventually, I came across another bench. This looked familiar. I had made it completely around the lake. I didn't want to do that. I consulted my map, read the directions, and realized I had missed a junction. I retraced my steps. Sigh.

I continued on. The path was so varied - some of it dirt, some gravel. Sometimes I could barely follow it because of the weedy overgrowth. It took me up and down and was rugged at times. Tiny toads hopped up onto the trail in front of me and welcomed me along the way. I passed over three small moss-covered stone bridges as I continued through the forest.

At one point, I noticed a narrow dirt trail that branched off the main one. I strayed down this tempting short path.

It led me to a bench that was painted in colorful autumn leaves with the words, "Peaceful Point" inscribed on the back of it. In front of the bench, a sign was posted by a wire fence which read, "Please do not harass the cows."

I sat for a while under a shady oak tree, but I didn't harass the cows that were lowing on the other side of the fence. I am a law-abiding citizen.

I got back on the trail and continued my trek. I was getting very tired. It seemed like I hadn't seen a human for a week. I finally reached the amphitheater (it is also on the National Register of Historic Places), so I knew I could bail and not continue with the next part of the hike, which, according to my book, would be a muddy one. This would be especially true after the storm we'd had.

I found myself on the loop on the paved park road. I had driven this the night before but had no idea how far away the parking lot for the Observation Tower, where my jeep was parked, was from here.

There was a woman walking up the road and I confirmed with her the direction of the parking lot. She said that it would be the first right turn down the road. The way she said it and nonchalantly flipped her hand, I was sure I'd find it just around the bend.

I didn't.

The walk along the road to the parking lot seemed longer than the three miles I had just hiked in the woods. I searched hopefully around each bend of the road for that brown sign with the arrow that would say, "Observation Tower", only to be disappointed time and time again.

Finally, there it was. I could have dropped to my knees and cried from happiness.

I staggered to my jeep, stripped off my knee brace, and threw my trek stick into the back. With the windows down, I grabbed a cold bottle of Diet Pepsi from my cooler and guzzled it, wishing it was a cold beer.

Later, I promised myself. Later.

What I learned today: Read directions.

Day 24

he worm I'd seen the day before was curled up and dead. All the back and forth motion and going nowhere had finally caused his demise.

"Was it you who gave me the firewood?" a woman asked me in the restroom.

"No, not me," I responded.

"Oh, well, I just used it for roasting marshmallows, that's all."

She was probably my age and had the kind of face that made you feel that you could trust her with your deepest secrets. I had noticed her, a newbie at the campground, the day before. She rode a motorcycle that was three times her size and pulled a tiny trailer.

She told me that she regularly traveled the country on her motorcycle. Her husband was a homebody, so she went it alone whenever the urge to hit the road struck her. Wow. I told her what I was doing, and she was duly impressed. We clicked immediately and must have chatted for 30 minutes or more. We talked about when we were kids and made "tents" by draping blankets over a couple of chairs in our living rooms. She said camping reminded her of playing house when she was a little girl. We swapped recommendations of campgrounds in Iowa, wished each other well, and said our goodbyes.

A pair of bunnies escorted me as I drove along the road out of the campground. I turned onto Highway 9 and headed west. A soft mist still hovered over the fields and the magnificent arms of wind turbines slowly turned on either side of the highway as I settled in for the drive to Northwest Iowa. I wanted to roll down my window, stick my head out, and let the wind rush through my hair like a happy puppy.

I decided to stay at Gull Point State Park in Milford, around the Okoboji area. I picked out a secluded site at the far end of the park. It was a shady spot and had no forest border. The campground layout was so winding and confusing that I felt like I needed to leave breadcrumbs to find my way to the showers.

Once I had my tent set up, I decided on an easy hike since the unsympathetic sun was already baking my fair skin. I had noticed a nature trail just across the road from the campgrounds, so I headed that way.

There were brochures in the box next to the trailhead, so I grabbed one and read through it. The brochure said that the Barney Peterson Memorial Interpretive Trail was about 1.5 miles long and that the land had been used as a golf course between 1917 and 1942. It closed in 1942 because of WW II. It reopened in 1946 for just a year and then was converted into a pasture until 1949. The Prairie Gold Boy Scout Council purchased the land in 1949 and operated a Boy Scout Camp on the property until 1974 when the Iowa Conservation Commission (now the Iowa DNR) bought it. Barney Peterson was employed by the Boy Scouts to help preserve this natural area, so the trail had been named in his memory.

Each area of interest along the trail had a numbered post and the brochure had corresponding information. Neat.

I wasn't far into the hike before I realized that I'd forgotten to apply insect repellent, but I felt too lazy to go back to my jeep and get it. What was a bite or two?

Mosquitos are not God's best creation. They buzzed, they whined, they whirred. They bit in the most troublesome spots. Behind my ear. In my ear. Behind my knee. On my elbow. Even on my butt. They showed no mercy. I think they saw me coming and cried with delight, "Lunch!"

They seemed to multiply like wire hangers do in coat closets.

I tried to outrun them but felt like I was the rabbit and they were the greyhounds.

I couldn't enjoy this trail because of these stinging pests. The 1.5-mile hike seemed like 15 miles.

Back at the campground, I took a shower and then decided to take a leisurely drive around the lake. When I got back to my campsite in the early evening, I feasted on roasted red pepper hummus, carrot sticks, and hot pepper cheese.

This was a quiet campground. There were several campers and RVs near the entrance, but only one across the road, and some distance from me. From what I could tell, I was the only tent in the park.

I hunted for twigs around my campsite and got a cozy fire started. I had just settled into my chair with a book and a beer when I heard a gurgling sound coming from the high weeds behind me. I got up to check out the area and discovered a small swamp hidden in the tall grasses. Great. Now I had to worry about a swamp monster with seaweed hanging from his mouth attacking me in the middle of the night. If it wasn't one thing, it was another.

Twilight was creeping in. Bullfrogs belched from the bog and birds were winding down their conversations. I felt intoxicated from my second beer and the flicker of the flames. As I watched a deer prance through the campground, I asked myself, "Could life possibly get any better?" Then I noticed how far away the outhouse was, and answered, "Yes."

I waited until the deer had roamed off and I'd sobered up before making the long trek to the restroom. I was glad I hadn't waited much longer, as the light was burned out inside. The embers in the fire pit were charred and ashen when I returned to my campsite. I settled onto my cot and thanked God for the blessings of the day.

I could hear the cicadas tune up for their nightly performance. They would be accompanied tonight by the gurgling and plopping of the bullfrogs in their marshy home. Every so often, I could hear the hum of the engine of a car on a nearby road.

And, of course, the buzz of a mosquito.

What I learned today: For every mosquito you kill, three more appear.

Day 25

I was on the road early to see the highest points in Iowa, the Ocheyedan Mound and the Sterler farm in Sibley.

The Ocheyedan was thought to be the state's highest point until 1970, when the U.S. Geological Survey discovered the mistake. The summit was actually 62 feet lower than had been previously thought. Three years of controversy ensued, and finally it was determined that the highest point, at 1670 feet was the Sterler farm.

I passed the small parking lot for the Ocheyedan Mound and had to turn around and go back. There wasn't a real trail to the top, only a worn footpath, sprinkled on both sides with purple prairie clover. It wasn't a high peak and didn't take but ten minutes or so to climb. The view was pretty, and I found myself wishing that I had packed a picnic (even at 8:00 a.m.).

I drove on to Sibley and was surprised to find that this family opened up their farm to visitors. I was the only one there so early in the day.

So now it was time to get some exercise. The only exercise I'd had the day before was running from mosquitos.

There was a long paved recreational trail all around the lake, but I preferred a wooded trail if I could find one. I consulted my hiking books and found Kettleson Hogsback Wildlife Management Area on the west side of Spirit Lake.

As usual, the directions and map from my books didn't match the actual trail at all.

This reminded me of my futile experiences with online dating. Often, the profile pictures didn't match the men when I met them in person. The profile picture of one of the first guys I met on match.com showed a tanned face, dark hair blowing in the breeze, and a perfect smile. He won me over with a note that said, "It would thrill me if you would respond to my message." We sent messages back and forth, and I enjoyed his witty personality. Soon we agreed to meet at a bookstore. He didn't look anything like his picture and I found him as dull as my statistics class in college.

About halfway into the hike, I came across a big orange box beside the lake. It reminded me of the devices placed along highways that warn you of your speed. I expected red lights to flash: "Your speed….20, 20, 19, 18…" as I slowed down to the acceptable speed limit. I think this contraption had something to do with pumping water.

This was good exercise, but an uneventful walk. I was starving, so I pulled a plastic container of hummus and a bag of carrot sticks out of the cooler in my jeep and had a nice snack before I moved on.

I still wanted more exercise, so I tried to find Horseshoe Bend Park. I found the park, but not the trails. I drove into a picnic area, hoping a trailhead would stem from there. A large wooden board was posted with a map of trails, but I couldn't make heads or tails out of it. I gave up.

I headed back to the campground to shower, and then off to Armstrong to visit an old friend.

Kim pulled off her catcher's mask and sauntered to the pitcher's mound. "Calm down," she said, as I risked

walking the runners around the bases. "*Just concentrate on the batter. You can do this.*"

Kim was a senior when I was a freshman in high school. She was one of my sister Nancy's best friends. I remember being so thrilled when they invited me to go out for a burger and malt at Pat & Mel's restaurant after a game in Kim's cool blue convertible. The restaurant has long since been razed and replaced by a Kum and Go convenience store.

I hadn't seen Kim in ten years, not since my mother's funeral. She was a retired teacher, living in Armstrong, and I wanted to surprise her with a visit.

I rang her door bell and heard the yapping of what was certainly a small, adorable dog. No answer. *She must be at work*, I thought. *I'll surprise her there.*

The newspaper office was located on the main street through town and I asked the woman behind the counter if Kim worked there. She said that she did, but she wasn't there now. I told her I was an old friend and had just come from Kim's house, but that she hadn't answered her door.

The woman pulled out her flip phone and offered to call her for me. Kim answered, and the woman handed her phone to me. "Kim! You didn't answer your door!" She had no idea who she was talking to, and I didn't tell her. "I'm coming back over. Will you answer the door this time?" A wary yes was her reply.

I pulled into her driveway for the second time and she met me in stocking feet at the door. She hadn't changed a bit. In fact, she hadn't changed since high school. She still had her long, straight blond hair and her same light blue eyes that couldn't hide a hint of mischief. Her smile hadn't changed either – warm and engaging.

Kim gave me a big hug and pulled me into her house. She said she had been napping when I'd stopped before, as her puppy was restless in the night and she hadn't slept at all.

Kim was understandably curious about why I was so far from home. She knew that I had moved back from New Hampshire, but what was I doing in Armstrong? I told her about my adventure and she said she couldn't handle the showers at campgrounds. I admitted that I had stepped on a few bugs. We both winced.

Kim asked if I wanted a snack. I remembered whenever Nancy and I visited Kim's home during high school, her mother always made sure that we were fed. She would greet us with a loving hug and immediately ask if we were hungry. Kim inherited her warm and caring nature from both her mother and father. They were two of the kindest people in town.

Kim rummaged in her pantry and refrigerator and filled up both arms with chips, crackers, and cheese and then dumped everything onto the kitchen table. Yum! My favorites!

Kim has an incredible home that could house a college sorority and she could write a book on do-it-your-self projects. Her basement was like a gymnasium, filled with all sorts of games and equipment for her great-nephews and nieces when they came to visit. Her rooms displayed Snoopy and froggy things, collections that surprised me and made her personality even more endearing. (I told her that I only collect dust and my thoughts every now and then.)

Eventually we moved out to the patio and the conversation topic turned to old boyfriends. Kim, like me, had never married. We talked about the perks of being single and at one point, said in perfect unison, "We can spend our money however we want" - after which, we high-fived each other.

We spent the entire afternoon and early evening catching up on our lives, families, and friends. There was never a lull in our conversation. I loved that.

The afternoon was turning into evening, and Kim suggested that we go out for dinner. She told me about places nearby, and said there were also a few places in Fairmont, Minnesota, which was just 18 miles away.

Wait a minute! Fairmont, Minnesota! You've got to be kidding me! I told Kim about growing up in Fairmont, Iowa and how every time I Googled it, Fairmont, MN popped up. Of course, I wanted to visit Fairmont, MN!

And my choice of restaurant? Perkins! They didn't have these in New England, at least not around where I lived, and I hadn't eaten at one since I'd returned to Iowa. Back in my wilder days, my drinking gal-pal Linda and I would go to Perkins after we'd closed the bars down and order a deli-ham-with-lots-of-cheese omelet, hash browns with cheese, and a jumbo blueberry muffin. After we'd licked our plates clean, we'd always make a pinky-pact that our diet would start immediately. We followed this routine every Saturday night.

When Kim and I returned from Fairmont and my nostalgic omelet meal, she showed me the county's Freedom Rock.

The Freedom Rocks are created by artist Ray "Bubba" Sorensen II to honor our veterans. They are painted murals on large boulders. It's Bubba's goal to have a Freedom Rock in all of Iowa's 99 counties. When the Armstrong Freedom Rock was put in place, there were already 49 counties that had rocks and 40 other counties booked to get one. Bubba often gets requests to mix ashes from veterans into the paint he uses.

The murals include portraits of fallen soldiers, the American flag, and a story from each county, among other touching tributes. I was amazed by the artwork and the meaningful purpose behind them.

Of course, Kim offered me a bed for the night, but I reminded her of my rules. I had so enjoyed seeing her again and hated for the day to end. But the park had a 10:30 curfew, so I had to get on the road.

What I learned today: Old friends are the best kind of friends.

~ ~ ~

"I'm lucky to be here, and I don't mean in this District, I mean on this earth."

I said this to the mediation board after I'd been called a "problem employee" by the Labor Relations Manager. (In the Postal Service, you are labeled a 'problem employee' when you file a discrimination case or fight for your rights.)

The Labor Relations Manager perked up. "What do you mean?" he said with a genuine note of concern in his voice.

"I wouldn't kill myself because I couldn't do that to my mother, but I think about cutting myself all the time."

Well, this changed the tone of the meeting altogether. After I admitted to six months of extensive therapy, relying on anti-depressant and anti-anxiety medication to get me through each day, and persistent thoughts of self-mutilation, Ms. Bobette finally apologized.

"It's too late for that," I cried and ran out of the room.

The Labor Relations Manager followed me to my office and tried to calm me. He called my initial Employee Assistance Program counselor, a blind therapist who amazed me with his ability to see. An immediate meeting was arranged.

I was later advised that the Performance Improvement Plan had been rescinded.

They expected me to pull the discrimination case I had filed. I did not. The case was settled out of court.

Day 26

I was excited to begin my trip through western Iowa and the Loess Hills. Sioux City marked the northern point of the Hills and that was where I was headed.

The Loess Hills were formed by deposits of very fine, windblown soil at the end of the last ice age. They span nearly 200 miles along western Iowa and into Missouri. You would have to travel to China to see a natural wonder similar to these.

Along the rural drive, I spotted a man who appeared to be "walking beans" in a soybean field. Boy, did that bring back memories. My brother and sisters and I did this in the summers during high school. It was a filthy job, walking through those wet, leafy fields, cutting out the weeds.

One day, in one of my uncle's fields, I grabbed onto a thick cornstalk and went to slice it with my sickle. I missed the stalk and made a deep gash in my leg instead.

That was the end of our work that day. Mother scolded my brother and sisters for not making a chair with their arms to carry me back through the field so I wouldn't have to walk with my leg bleeding so. I remember lying on my back in the doctor's office watching him roughly scrub the dirt from the wound before he stitched it up. Seven stitches, still a scar.

Recently, I asked my uncle about bean walking. He said it isn't done so much anymore because of improved herbicides that keep weeds from growing in the soybean fields. But it was sure good money for us back then.

The drive to Stone State Park took most of the morning. The campground was small, and the tent area was on a hill up above the RV and camper section. *Oh no*, I thought. *I'm setting myself up for another critter attack.* I decided to chance it and paid for three nights. There were a lot of good hiking trails in this park and I guessed I would need at least three days to discover them all. I set up my tent and set off to find my first trailhead.

I had difficulty finding the trailhead from the instructions given in the book. I finally noticed a sign along the road with my brown hiker man on it, so I parked my jeep by a shelter and walked to the trailhead. After a short distance, a sign indicated two trails. I decided to take the Mount Lucia Trial. It had a steep incline right off the bat that really got my heart pumping. This trail was a combination of dirt, gravel, horse manure, up and down, shade, and sun: a little bit of everything, and it tested my strength and determination.

When I reached the top, there were four riders on horses under the shade trees. The trails in this park were popular among equestrians. I guess I could have figured this out by the evidence they left behind.

After the riders had left, I took a breather on a bench overlooking the Iowa countryside. There was a brass plate on the bench, which I expected to be some sort of dedication. It read, "For Jim, because he is old and likes to sit." Yes, I guess that was some sort of dedication.

This was supposed to be a loop trail, *according to my map*, so I took another path down, thinking it would complete the loop. It wasn't long before the signs on the trail pointed out the error of my ways. I had to retrace my steps and take my original path back to the trailhead. I needed to burn these damn books.

The heat was really starting to get to me, but the temperature was only in the mid-80s. I had hiked in warmer weather on this trip. I was even starting to feel a little faint. I told myself that I'd feel better after I showered and got something to eat.

I walked into the shower at the campground and was met with an odor like nothing I could describe. I turned up my nose like The Beaver when he ate Brussels sprouts for the first time.

I kicked aside a few bugs on the shower floor and flicked a daddy-long-legs off the shower curtain. Ugh.

The mellow vibe of the evening matched my weary mood. I built a soothing fire and settled into my chair. I didn't have the energy to even hold a book, so I got out my CD player and listened to one instead.

The sun's last rays filtered through the trees as I unzipped my tent. Another good day of hiking. I was so lucky. I was so pooped.

What I learned today: Kim was right about campground showers.

Day 27

*W*ith their lighthearted chirping, the songbirds were urging me to get my day started. I unzipped my tent, stepped out, stretched, and blinked my eyes against the early morning sun.

Five Ridge Prairie is northwest of Sioux City, on the far reaches of Loess Hills. It's named for the five ridges that dissect the preserve and is a mixture of prairie and woodland. It sounded just like my type of trail, so I took off, anxious for a day of good hiking.

The trailhead was way out in the boondocks. Was it safe for me to be out here alone? I pulled into the parking area and three deer skipped across the high grass in front of me.

I went through my normal prep and tucked the trail map from my guide book into the waistband of my shorts. The guide warned that "steep climbs could make this hike difficult for some."

The trail started out with a steep decline. I knew what this meant. The road was rough, an old mowed farm road that made walking difficult. The clumps of dried mowed grass were stiff and uneven. I finally got to a junction that had a map box, which was, of course, empty. A post signaled R1 with an arrow one way and R2 with an arrow another way. Neither matched the map I had. Oh boy.

I took the left road which soon turned into a narrow footpath that led me up and up and up to the most incredible view. Wildflowers swayed recklessly around me. Butterflies flirted with each other and songbirds welcomed me to their paradise. Skinny grasshoppers popped along the path. I dropped my backpack, twirled around, and burst into song, "The hills are alive with the sound of music!". Well, at least that's what I felt like doing.

Again, I was astonished that Iowa contained such simple, innocent beauty. I wanted to stay here all day and just be awed.

But eventually, I had a decision to make. Did I want to continue with the trail? I looked at the steep drop in the path ahead of me. Or should I head back? I rummaged in my backpack for a coin to flip. None.

So, I flipped my empty soda bottle. If it landed upright, I would go on. If it landed on its side, I'd head back.

I flipped it high into the air.

Then I gathered my backpack and headed back the way I'd come. Toward the end, when the trail became steep, I kept my head down and just concentrated on taking it one step at a time. Looking ahead at the long uphill scramble seemed discouraging. The guidebook wasn't kidding when it warned of these climbs.

When I got back to my jeep, sweaty and exhausted, I thought that an afternoon in the laundromat sounded inviting and relaxing. I was out of clean socks.

I thought I would quickly check out another trailhead in the park before my laundromat trip. I parked on the side of the road to reach the trailhead and set off on a trail called "Broken Toe".

I started out on the flat path with a spring in my step, thinking that this matched my energy level perfectly. Well now, how things change. The hike became brutal. And the mounds of fresh horse manure that I had to climb over had me huffing and puffing too.

Why had I abandoned the idea of a quiet afternoon in an air-conditioned laundromat listening to the purr of a dryer, for this? Was I mad?

The trail mocked me with posts at half-mile intervals. I had wanted a simple, short hike, but now that I was on this darn trail, for some reason I felt compelled to see it through. Finally, I could see blue sky. There was an end to this trail after all. Thank you, God! I mustered the energy to get to the top, started humming the tune from the movie, *Rocky*, and danced around with my arms in the air.

I dropped my body onto the bench for weary hikers and squinted my eyes at the scorching sun. Circling black birds were waiting directly above me. Buzzards? Not yet...

I got up and looked at the sign that indicated the different trails and distances. What the heck? 1.8 miles for the Broken Toe Trail? Almost two miles back to my jeep? I wanted to click my heels three times like Dorothy in *The Wizard of Oz*, and magically be transported down to the road.

I took a deep sigh, a swig of my soda, and started off. I promised myself a cold beer as a reward when I got back to my campsite. I think I became a little delirious as I began to talk to myself on the trek down. The birds cocked their heads in amusement at my mutterings.

The campground had filled up by the time I returned. I showered and built myself a roaring fire. As promised,

I had a couple of cold beers after the strenuous day of hiking. It had been the toughest so far, and completely unintentional.

As I felt the hush of the evening surround me, I realized that it took so little to make me so happy, so content - a warm crackling fire, a good book in my lap, a cold beer in my hand, twinkling stars above me, fire-flies around me.

What I learned today: Stick to Plan A.

Day 28

I bet that underneath Rick's high school senior year-book picture it reads, "Most likely to ride the most consecutive RAGBRAIs".

RAGBRAI stands for "Register's Annual Great Bike Ride Across Iowa", and this was year 17 for Rick. For that, he deserved a trophy or a t-shirt or a case of beer or a standing ovation or something.

Rick and I met in Chicago some 30 years ago, at what was then our Regional Sales Office for the Postal Service. He was in the Marketing Department in Sioux City, and I was in Marketing in Des Moines. We were both Account Managers at the time and were there for some sort of training or conference. I noticed that he was really cute and drove a motorcycle. When the conference was over, he invited me to Sioux City and we water-skied along the Missouri River.

We connected again through Facebook after I'd moved back to Iowa, six months before I took off on this journey. His birthday was a few days before mine and he made the long drive from Yankton, South Dakota, where he is now living, to do a pub crawl along Court Avenue in Des Moines with me.

Rick is a fun guy, no doubt about it. He will go along with just about anything. So, when I suggested that we play a game during our pub crawl, he was all in. (I was already three sheets to the wind when I suggested this.) We had to guess the name of our waiter/waitress/ bartender, and whoever came closest, won. Huh?

Now, after spending too many days alone in the woods, I was in the mood for a little male companion- ship. I texted Rick, "I'm camping at Stone State Park in Sioux City the next couple of nights. Wanna sing campfire songs with me?"

His response came within the hour: "Heck yes."

I sent him my camp site number and he asked if I was with a group or by myself. I responded, "Just me. I'm on an adventure."

I was on my second beer and reading in my chair when I got a text from Rick saying that he was half an hour out from joining my adventure. A few minutes later, I looked up to see a dusty SUV pull in beside my jeep.

Rick looked the same. Tall as a corn stalk, broad-shouldered, sexy, with not an ounce of fat on his athletic 61-one-year old frame. His mischievous smile combined with his impossible indigo blue eyes could charm any girl. He was one of the most mild-manned men that I knew, and I bet the earth would shake if he would ever lose his temper. Gosh, he looked good.

I stood and gave him a hug. "Geez, that was a quick half hour," I teased. "Reception must be bad out here."

I got a beer for him from the cooler and then apologized for the Michelob Ultra, remembering that he refers to this brand as "water". Still, we shared a couple of bottles together while I told him about my adventure so far.

Rick told me all about how he had been spending his time since retirement, arranging kayak and bicycle tours. He had converted a big bus to accommodate these tours, complete with a toilet and shower. He teased that it was too bad I didn't bike, otherwise he would marry me.

Rick said that he was also a caretaker for a 94-year old man. He pulled up a picture on his phone of them eating breakfast together at a restaurant. "Which one is you?" I asked with a wink.

A small, ugly car pulled into the site several spots down from us, and a young couple got out. A pretty brunette in a polka-dot dress with low-heeled black pumps began to pitch a condo-tent while her pot-bellied man mulled about. Soon, she came over to our site and asked if we had change for a twenty. I detected an English accent, so I asked where she was from. "Chicago," was her reply. She said they were headed to the Black Hills for vacation, so Rick filled her in on all the tourist attractions. She thanked us with a smile that showed more gum than teeth and went back to her task.

I watched her walk away with her polka-dot dress swishing with each step. I looked down at my simple white t-shirt, Hawaiian-print draw-string cotton capri pants, and Sketcher flip-flops. Had I been doing this wrong all along? I wondered if I was underdressed for camping life.

The night was but a pup, so we decided to go bar-hopping along the river. The only food on the menu at the first place was mac and cheese pizza, so we had a beer and moved on.

We ordered food at the second place. My chicken finger basket came with seasoned French fries. I couldn't remember the last time that I'd had French fries. I bathed those puppies in ketchup and savored every bite.

I invited Rick to come back to Des Moines for our birthdays again this year and suggested we should go to the State Fair. I was astonished that he'd never been to the Fair. This was just wrong. This was one of my very favorite things to do, and I couldn't think of anyone I knew from Iowa who hadn't been there. Rick asked what was so great about it.

"Oh My God! Rick! The Iowa State Fair was in the book of 100 things to do before you die! You must go! The corn dogs with mustard, the Bud Tent, the nachos with extra jalapeno peppers, the double Ferris wheel after dark, the photography exhibit, the people watching, the hog-calling contest, the biggest boar, the fantastic free entertainment, the real lemonade…should I go on? It is just tragic that you haven't been to the Fair."

Rick seemed unimpressed.

Then we got to talking about ziplining, and I told him I really wanted to go on the zipline in Alaska.

"Hey! We should road-trip to Alaska! Wouldn't that be fun, Rick? Let's go at the end of September before it gets too cold. They say you really get to know a person when you take a road trip with them," I teased.

Rick didn't seem to share my enthusiasm for this trip, and said that he would have to see if he could "work it in."

We pulled into the campground, and Rick brushed his teeth at the water pump nearby. (He'd had an onion on his Anchor Burger at the restaurant.)

We rested our backs across from each other on the picnic table benches and watched the fireflies dance across the dark sky. No words were spoken between us. I knew that I hadn't sold Rick on ziplining in Alaska and probably not even the State Fair. But watching this quiet light show together was enough.

Too soon, Rick rose and said he should go. He had an hour drive ahead of him. He gave me a warm hug and a few sweet kisses. While in his embrace, I spotted the first star in the sky. "Star light, star bright, first star I see tonight, I wish I may, I wish I might, have this wish I wish tonight."

I gently pulled away from Rick and said, "I don't have anything to wish for, Rick. I have everything I want." I could hear his smile in the quiet darkness that surrounded us.

I told him I was going to drive to the campground restroom. He was gone when I returned to my site. I went through my normal bedtime routine, but somehow, tonight, it all seemed a little lonely.

I looked up again at the stars. And then I made a wish.

What I learned today: A cold beer on a hot summer night with an old friend is a comfortable kind of bliss.

~ ~ ~

The next postal shake-up involved consolidation. The District of New Hampshire was consolidating with the District of Maine.

I had to compete for my same position, but since that position hadn't previously existed in Maine, I was confident that I would be the successful candidate. I knew there weren't many applicants in the package as everyone assumed that I would be a shoo-in for the job.

All affected employees were supposed to hear about their job placements on a pre-determined Friday. My counterparts and I were keeping in touch with each other all day, our nerves on end.

In the Postal Service, bad news was always delivered at the end of the day. As I watched the clock tick toward 4:30, I knew my phone call would not be good news.

It wasn't.

Not only did I not get "my" job, but I also didn't get either of the other two jobs that I'd applied for. This was really bad.

I was marked in the District for my previous discrimination complaint. They might as well have slapped a big scarlet letter on my chest. (I discovered later that Ms. Bobette had influenced the selection.)

My impressive career background didn't mean squat. I was scared now. If I didn't get placed in the next round, I wouldn't have a job. There would be plenty of postmaster positions open in Vermont, New Hampshire, and Maine. Would I have to settle for one of those? I *hated* being a postmaster! It would be a fate worse than death. But it would be a job.

I don't remember the drive home from work that day. I was so humiliated that I didn't know how I could possibly face any of my peers again. I had held this job for years, not only in New Hampshire, but also in Des Moines. Everyone would be talking. I so yearned for the safety of Mother's skirts to shield me from this frightening world.

Once home, I called the Employee Assistance Program hotline with tears in my eyes and a knife in my hand.

Day 29

S weet! I found another Goodwill store on my way out of Sioux City. I stopped in and bought two hard cover books for $5.00. The elderly, gray-haired cashier totaled up my purchase and announced the amount due. She cheerfully said, "That's with the senior discount. You are over 62, right?"

I jumped over the counter as swiftly as an Olympic athlete would clear a hurdle, pinned her against the wall, and muttered between clenched teeth, "Who you calling 'over 62', lady?"

Actually, I politely said, "I have a way to go before I hit 62."

"Oh!" she said. "I didn't mean to insult you. I'll give you the discount anyway." She gave me an apologetic smile and handed me my purchase.

"Thanks," I mumbled as I took my bag and left the store.

When I got into my jeep, I flipped the visor down and studied my reflection in the mirror. I noticed the graying hair around my temples. It was time for a dye job. Makeup could no longer cover the deep lines around my eyes and mouth. And I had more chins than a Chinese phone book. The lady was right. I looked older than 62.

My brother always had said that Andy Williams would sing at his wedding. Sadly, Andy died, and my brother never got married.

President Ronald Reagan declared Andy Williams' voice a national treasure. I believe it was. I have a collection of his vinyl records. So, I couldn't make a tour of the great state of Iowa without visiting Wall Lake, the town where Andy was born and raised.

The house where he grew up was only open for tours two hours a week: on Sundays from 2:00 to 4:00. I was so glad I happened to be in the area on a Sunday.

I was greeted by two elderly women who got up from their seats in the parlor when I walked into the old white house. They kindly asked for a contribution of $3.00 for a tour of the house and gave me a magnet when I stuffed three one-dollar bills into the plastic cylinder on top of an oak roll-top desk.

I signed my name in a guest book and then looked around the house. I was actually standing where this famous musician had grown up. Wow.

One of the ladies took over my private tour and told me all about Andy's early years in Wall Lake. I drank it all in. I had read his autobiography, *Moon River and Me*, years ago, but didn't remember much.

I took my time perusing the old pictures of Andy and The Williams Brothers that were displayed on the wall. I loved this.

I asked to see the gift shop, thinking I could find a memento for my brother. The woman apologized that the shop was a little short on inventory and took me into the shed next door. There were just a few of his albums displayed on the wall and note cards and postcards in a basket. I bought a postcard for a quarter.

I thanked her for sharing her knowledge and time with me as I said my goodbye. She told me to come again, which I doubted I would.

I got into my jeep and penned a quick note to my brother on the postcard. I put a stamp on it and dropped it into the postal collection box on my way out of town.

That was the best I could do, bro'. I was keeping the magnet for myself.

The detour off my tour I was looking forward to the most was to spend time with my nephew Kevin, the youngest son of my oldest sister Mary. He had finished his first year teaching high school in Storm Lake. I had been gone for fifteen years and missed most of his life. This would be the first time that I had spent one-on-one time with him, ever, and I was really looking forward to getting to know him.

We met for dinner at one of his favorite Mexican restaurants. Kevin has a face that will never age. His eyes brightened when he talked about something that he was passionate about, like writing. I'd no idea that he liked to write. And I'd also had no idea that he is terrified of alligators. How did he develop that fear? In Iowa, no less.

We had the most pleasant dinner, never a lull in our conversation. I felt like I'd gotten to know my nephew a little better, but more importantly, I felt like I'd made a new friend.

There was an early evening calm in the air when I returned to my campsite. I was staying at a camp-ground just across from the lake. I walked across the road, settled onto a bench, and watched the graceful setting of the sun.

I reluctantly let the exhilaration of another summer day slowly drift away.

What I learned today: Trust the presumptions of Goodwill cashiers. It will earn you a 10% discount.

Day 30

I t was already 75 degrees at 6:45 a.m. Not a good sign. Sweat dripped from my face and onto the canvas of my tent as I pulled it down. Ugh. I decided not to shower - what was the point?

The campground hadn't woken yet. I slowly drove through the RVs and campers and noticed how some had even brought large potted plants from home to set outside their campers. Really?

The sun was negotiating with the clouds when I turned onto Highway 71. As I marveled at the color surrounding me, vivid golds and greens and yellows, it occurred to me that I had become less preoccupied by thoughts of my regrettable past as my journey progressed. Was I finally finding peace? Was the fog finally lifting?

It was a long, pretty drive along Highway 30 to Honey Creek and the Hitchcock Nature Center, where I planned on camping the next three nights. I made three loops through the campground before I found the tent camping area. Several secluded sites were located down a steep hill, buried in the woods.

I loved it.

But I was also scared. It was too remote.

The level site I wanted had bread and other garbage strewn about by the previous campers. This would surely lure critters. And did I really want to lug my tent and equipment all the way down here?

I decided to check out another campground in Missouri Valley.

The Wilson Island State Recreational Area campground was the biggest I had seen on my adventure. I was surprised only a few campers were staying here and just one other tent camper. Perfect. I set up in a shady spot and drove back down to the Nature Center to do some hiking.

The Hitchcock Nature Center charged a $2.00 entrance fee that you just put into an envelope at the gate. I sealed the envelope and made my way along the narrow road to find the Badger Ridge trailhead, which was supposed to be next to the lodge. I shouldn't have any trouble finding this one.

It was 92 degrees when I stepped onto the dirt trail, which started out with a steep descent. I wouldn't like this at all on the way back.

The single-lane path stretched up and down along a narrow ridge, and the brutal sun beat down on me almost the entire way. But the view of the planted fields and the Loess Hills below kept me going. Despite feeling like I was suffocating from the heat, I made it to the top of an overlook where there was a bench where I could rest. I shrugged off my backpack and let it drop to the ground. Then I sank onto the bench and just stared at the beauty of the land. I felt like I was on top of the world. I was reminded of JRR Tolkien's quote, "Do not spoil the wonder with haste." I sat back and savored the view. I had no place I had to be.

I finally got up enough energy to bend over and unzip my backpack to retrieve my bottle of iced tea. It was warm, but it didn't matter. My lips were so parched, my mouth as dry as the Sahara Desert.

I looked at the path before me. I so wanted to continue.

But my stomach was starting to feel queasy. Oh no.

The only other time in my life I remember fainting was in high school marching band. We were dressed in full uniform and were lined up at the back parking lot of the high school, ready to practice. I must have gone all wobbly in the knees, for the next thing I knew, my sister Mary had her arm firmly around my shoulder and was leading me to the grassy bank off the parking lot and easing me onto the ground.

I didn't want to go all wobbly in the knees atop this hill. I didn't want rescue units to have to put me on a stretcher and jerk me away by helicopter. Nope. I had to turn back.

I cursed myself on the hike back for not fueling my body better before I'd set off.

Just one foot in front of the other, I thought as I slowly staggered along the trail. I looked down at my aluminum trek stick and could have sworn that it had steam coming off it. The mosquitoes must even have felt sorry for me, because I didn't even feel one light on my clammy skin.

The weather channel on my iPhone said it was ninety-five degrees and warned an "excessive heat watch" was in effect. What the heck? I had never heard of that before.

When I made it down, I headed to the local grocery store and strolled through the aisles, my clothes sticking to me like Saran Wrap. At the check-out counter, I looked at the contents of my cart: a six-pack of Michelob Ultra, a six-pack of Diet Pepsi, a box of spinach and garlic Good Thins crackers, four mini packs of Wholly Guacamole, and a small package of Tostitos nacho cheese dip. Yum.

Back at the campground, I took a nice shower. It was again too hot to dry my hair. My cotton dress was soaked with sweat soon after I put it on. I sat in the shade, drank a few cold beers, and thought about snowstorms.

Damn. It was hot.

What I learned today: There is no shade on the top of the world.

Day 31

A gentle thunderstorm rolled through during the night, but it was nothing raging like I'd had experienced before. Hopefully, this would cool things off a bit. I remembered that I had left a couple of my sweaty bras hanging on my lawn chair to dry off. The rain had laundered them for me!

I unzipped my tent a little after 7:00 and the air smelled so fresh, so pure. I dodged the huge rain puddles and jumped into my jeep. I was looking forward to hiking Preparation Canyon.

The sky was a hazy, misty blue as I drove along the backroads. Along the way, I stopped for a wild turkey to scoot off the road in front of me. I hadn't seen one of these since I'd left New Hampshire, where they were common visitors to my backyard.

The wood board inside the park entrance had a box containing trail maps. I also had the map from my guide book. Still, I must have driven more than an hour looking for the damn trailhead. Back and forth and back and forth I drove, trying to make sense of Peach Ave.

I finally gave up and settled for a wooded hike that I stumbled across within the park called Sarah's Trail. No majestic vistas. The trail was overgrown, and weedy vegetation was dense around my feet. And of course, an annoying mosquito followed me the entire way. It was a nice walk, but I really wanted views. After some time, I turned around and decided to find a trail that offered more. When I got back to my jeep, I had to pick sticky green plants off my clothing. What the heck?

I drove northwest to Onawa and took the guide-book's directions to the Sylvan Runkel State Preserve. There were two trailhead options and I struck out on both. I found the first one, but it was just prairie. I could find no discernable trail. I couldn't find the second trail-head at all, even after checking and rechecking the direc-tions and driving and turning around again and again. *When was this guidebook published? 20 years ago?*

What a wasted morning. How disappointing.

Plan C: Head back to the Hitchcock Nature Center.

I paid the $2.00 entrance fee to the center and made my way back towards the lodge, where I had been the day before. I looked at the board that mapped out all the trails and saw that the Fox Run Ridge trail was labeled "easy". Perfect, as the pain in my hip was killing me.

Early into the hike, I questioned who rated the trail. Their definition of easy was certainly different than mine.

I reached a high overlook called "Angel's Dead End" and settled onto a bench, letting the calming breeze whisper about me. A string of dirt-trodden paths sprawled below me, winding through the tall trees, all of them seducing me with their mysterious destinations. I felt the cool breath of God on my neck, the soft sigh of an angel in my ear. I felt calm, like a spiritual spell had been cast upon me.

Pulling me from my trance, a young man spurted up and skidded to a stop in the gravel next to me, surprised by my presence.

"Don't tell me you're jogging this trail," I said. The kid wasn't even sweating, and I looked like I'd just come out of the steam room at the gym.

"Yeah, I come here all the time on my lunch break," he responded. "I live in Omaha."

"Lucky you to have all this in your backyard." I gestured at the trodden paths below us.

His sprouting whiskers and dark locks were cute, and I immediately wanted to introduce him to my niece Michelle.

He asked if I was from Iowa and I said yes. He said he'd heard that there were some awesome caves in Iowa.

"Yes, if you like to crawl on your belly. Me? Not so much."

He introduced himself, shook my hand, and said it was nice meeting me. Then he bounded off. Ah, to be young again.

I got up and continued to hobble along the trail. I wished I had a bullet to bite for the pain in my hip. Twice, I considered turning around. I was so glad I didn't. The overlook at the end of the trail was about the most stunning view I have ever seen. I dropped my backpack and my jaw and stared. A photograph could never capture the raw and perfect beauty of this sight.

I sat for a while on the ground looking out over the neat patchwork of fields. I'd seen majestic mountains. I'd seen deep blue oceans. I'd seen towering waterfalls. I'd seen picturesque lighthouses. But this, this simple Iowa countryside had them all beat.

Back at camp, I showered and ate a light supper. It had turned out to be a good day. The sensational hike in the afternoon had compensated for the disappointing morning.

I did a little reading before I retired to my chamber for the evening. I realized I'd come to depend on the cicadas lulling me to sleep every night. It reminded me of listening to their songs on the porch swing on the farm when I was a small girl. Their melodies ignited such sweet memories.

What I learned today: I wouldn't call myself stupid. I just have really bad luck when it comes to finding trailheads.

~ ~ ~

Yes, my driver observations (spying on carriers to make sure they were following proper safety procedures) were up to date. Yes, I had given and recorded weekly safety talks on the District's website. Yes, I had done an investigation of the scene of the accident and taken pictures. Yes, I had completed the mountain of paperwork involved and submitted the pile to the District Safety Office.

The teleconference with District personnel after an accident was the worst part of being a postmaster. They drilled you. It was as if you had been in the accident, not one of your employees. All postmasters who had experienced an accident in their office during the preceding week would receive an invitation to attend the teleconference. And they had better be prepared.

Once, I was so humiliated by the way I was treated by top management on a teleconference because my discipline to the employee wasn't strict enough that I wanted to hang up and walk out the back door. What happened to treating each other with respect?

This particular accident involved one of my senior rural carriers. While traveling along a gravel road, he was distracted by barking dogs, swerved across the road, and hit a tree.

This carrier was in the wrong profession. His mother and wife had both been killed in automobile accidents, and he therefore had a fear of driving - yet this job required driving, six days a week. Go figure. His current wife brought him to work and picked him up every day. The massive volume increase in packages during December sent him over the edge every year and he went out of work on stress leave.

I disconnected from the conference call after being ordered by the great powers at the District to give this employee a Letter of Warning for his inattention. I was surprised that they did not demand I issue a seven-day suspension.

I slumped back into my swivel chair and stared at the three-month calendar on the wall of my office. It mocked me. It constantly reminded me that my life was slipping away like grains of sand in an hour glass. How much longer was I simply going to settle for days filled with rescuing employees when their vehicles broke down, chasing down lost packages, correcting misdelivered mail, dealing with childish and disrespectful employees, and surviving in a career that continued to hold no meaning for me whatsoever?

It was time to go.

It was time to start living.

I had a doctor's note that put me out of work indefinitely for the painful arthritis in my right hand that was exasperated by the repetitive motion of sorting mail. I had six months of sick leave accrued that I was planning on using before I officially retired. I counted and recounted the days. April 7th and I was gone. Back home to Iowa where I belonged.

My boss never said goodbye or wished me well in my retirement. After thirty-eight years of dedicated service. Shameful.

I so needed a carefree adventure. My spirit was crushed. I needed to shake off the emotional abuse that I had suffered along the path of my career. I needed to rebuild my self-worth, which had been shattered and now lay in pieces at my feet.

I had to salvage the person that my job had beat out of me. She was there somewhere.

I was going to find her.

Day 32

*I*t was 6:00 a.m. and the temperature had already reached 77 degrees. Oh my. My plan was to revisit the Badger Ridge Trail at the Hitchcock Nature Center before it got too hot, then head south to my next destination, Sidney.

I was glad that the Nature Center opened early. I seemed to be the only visitor. I was anxious to see the trail through this time, as I'd so enjoyed the portion that I had hiked the other day.

The brochure at the trailhead said this trail was "moderate" in difficulty, and it was true to its word. It twisted up and down, through prairie, hills, and timber. The beauty of this trail was like no other. I felt like I was in a fairy glen, like I had stepped into another world. The path was mostly dirt and very narrow in most places. It ended at a primitive campsite sheltered by trees where I rested before starting my trek back.

The spot was so peaceful and quiet. I could have stayed there forever.

As I reached the overlook on my return, I saw a solitary deer grazing in the field below. I smiled at the simple loveliness of this scene.

The hike turned out to be rather short. I was done at 8:10, so I hit the road for Sidney. I thought it would take about two hours to get there.

The Waubonsie State Park campground was a small one. I was the only tent camper, and there were only three or four other RV campers set up. I picked out a site and set up my tent. I thought I could handle another short hike before the real heat hit in the afternoon.

The wood board at the trailhead had a box that said, "Trail Brochures, Take One". The box was empty. I folded the map and directions that I'd torn from one of my hiking books and set off on the Bridge Trail.

Why hadn't I read about this trail before I'd started it? It was torture. Portions of it were washed out, making my progress slow and deliberate. I wasn't seeking a good workout. Not in this blasted heat.

There weren't any signs on the trail, so I tore up clumps of weeds and placed them in the middle of the path, so I'd know which forks to take on my return. It was not the most sophisticated method but darn it! If there weren't signs and the maps in the books confused me, I would make my own pointers.

I continued on. Sweat dripped from the tips of my nose and chin and left a wet dotted trail on the dirt path.

At one point, I looked up at the muddy, rutted incline facing me and wished I had the cord from the Fenelon Elevator to pull to get me to the top. I took a deep breath and began the climb. No wonder no one else was on this trail. I was the only fool.

And the mosquitos. I'd doused myself with insect repellant before entering the woods, yet still I heard a relentless buzzing at my ear. I wondered if the same mosquito followed me from trail to trail, or if a tiny baton was handed off in each park. Maybe it was a mosquito mafia that was out to get me. Sometimes I waved my hand so hard to shoo away these irritating insects that I lost my balance and almost fell over.

I crawled back to my jeep around noon. I figured I must have lost half my body weight on that short, treacherous hike. I had been sucked of my energy and my blood. All I wanted was to find the nearest Dairy Queen, plop myself down in the middle of the floor, and eat chocolate ice cream the rest of the day.

I showered in the cleanest shower of all the campgrounds I'd stayed in. I didn't want to put clothes back on because I knew I would sweat through them right away. I did.

I had no food, so I made a drive into town and bought a deli sandwich from Casey's. With mayo. And Pop Chips. Diet Pepsi even seemed too heavy to drink in this heat, so I got the biggest cup of iced tea they sold. I brought this all back to my campsite and had myself a little picnic in the shade.

The rest of the day would be spent reading in the coolest spot I could find. Even my cheater glasses had steamed over from the heat. The flies were biting, but I didn't want to spray myself with insect repellent as it was slick and icky. I decided to retire to my tent where the insects wouldn't pester me.

I must have dozed off for a while, because it was 4:00 when I woke up, and even though a nice breeze was blowing through the flap of my tent, I was still soaked with sweat. I checked my iPhone and the temperature said 96 degrees, but *"feels like 110 degrees"*. No kidding.

Ice cream. *I had to have ice cream!*

With great effort, I pulled myself off my sweat-soaked cot and stumbled to my jeep. Ahhh, the air conditioning felt so good. I cranked it on full blast.

Hamburg was a small town in the southwestern corner of the state, just a mile or so from the Missouri border. It was only six miles from Waubonsie State Park, but it seemed like 60 miles. After paying for my chocolate chip ice cream sandwich, I raced to my jeep, practically tearing down the Casey's door. I had that creamy treat consumed by the time I pulled out of the parking lot. I have never enjoyed ice cream so much in my life.

I noticed that there was another Freedom Rock in the park next to Casey's. I licked each finger to make sure I had captured every cookie crumb of my ice cream treat, and then got out of my jeep to marvel at this painted wonder.

Back at the campground, there was no sign of life. I assumed they were all in town getting ice cream.

I settled in, less cranky now that I'd had my ice cream fix. Sweat dripped off my chin and onto my book as I read. My iPhone showed a moving red banner at the top of the weather channel's screen that advised of the excessive heat warning.

I remembered my rules - I couldn't pack up and check in to a hotel unless tornado sirens were blaring. Hmm, my rules didn't say anything about an excessive heat warning. Hmm. Should I?

Naw.

It was 8:30 p.m., and I tried to get comfortable in my tent. My t-shirt was soaked, and I had just put it on. I wiped the sweat off my face with a wash towel and begged for a breeze to come through the open flap of the tent. I would have slept outside if I wasn't so afraid of any critters that might have been lurking nearby.

What I learned today: I needed to have my head examined for hiking such a brutal trail in 100-degree weather.

Day 33

*D*awn had finally come.

It had been the most miserable night of my trip. The nervous chattering of insects from the trees began at dusk and had continued until dawn. I had never heard this noise before, but it was loud and constant and as irritating to me as the snapping of gum. I wished I had the power of Fonzie in a *Happy Days* episode where he simply sat up from his sleeping bag and said, "Cool it!" to silence the sounds of nature.

I had woken several times during the night to the sound of the wind whipping against my tent. At least I think it was the wind.

Some other unknown insect had tried desperately to get my attention in the early morning hours by calling, "Zeet! Zeet!" under the canopy of my tent. I was so hot and tired that I didn't care what it was. It could gnaw through my tent and eat me alive for all I cared.

With just a few snippets of sleep, I hoped I would have the energy I would surely need for the hike that I'd planned for the morning. I wanted to get an early start as I knew it would be another blistering day.

The promise of majestic vistas motivated me as I made my way to the trailhead in Waubonsie State Park. I had changed into the most lightweight clean clothes that I had, pulled a cap down over my eyes, and went through the normal routine of strapping on my knee brace, packing my backpack with a sweaty bottle of ice tea, my camera, notepad, and pencil. I tucked the hiking map into the waistband of my shorts, adjusted my trek stick, and with a heavy sigh, set out. It was 7:00 a.m.

As usual, I didn't meet anyone on the trail. It was a roller-coaster walk through the woods, just the kind I like. Then after about two miles and a heck of an incline, I reached the promised overlook. I could see Kansas, Missouri, Nebraska, and Iowa. I settled myself on a bench and thought about how lucky I was to live in such a great state and to be able to hike to this place to see such rich beauty.

The rest of the hike was grueling. I needed a machete to fight my way through the overgrowth. Soon the hike went downhill, literally and figuratively. The path turned into a steep, small groove that had been washed out. I clutched my stick tightly as I negotiated it, but I still had to hang on to tree branches on my way. I couldn't believe I didn't take a fall - it was that steep and slick.

As I hiked down, down, down, I knew that eventually I would have to come back up, up, up. Yep.

I returned to my jeep, my entire body slick with sweat. As I folded up my stick and unstrapped my brace, I knew this had been my last hike. I was bitten, bruised, and bone-tired. It was time to go home.

After I showered, I began the drive back to Des Moines.

With a wistful smile, I turned my jeep onto Interstate 35. My adventure was over. Thirty-three days of hiking and discovering the state where I had been born and raised.

I folded the creased and tattered Iowa map that had served me so well and tucked it into the pocket of the door. I wouldn't need this again.

Reflections

What I learned in life:

Often, I found myself on an unfamiliar path, unsure of which way to turn. Sometimes I took one road to find that it wasn't the right one for me, that it didn't lead me to where I wanted to go so I had to turn back and try another one.

There were times in my life when the path ahead was terrifying. I had to focus on getting through just one day at a time.

Many times, I found myself in a dark place and I didn't think I could find my way out, but with perseverance and resolve I continued and emerged stronger and more determined.

I met many obstacles along my life's journey. I had to find ways to step around them and continue on.

I learned that it was important to work through pain and not give up. I often stumbled along life's journey, found myself bruised and beaten, but I dusted myself off and I got on my feet again.

And, when I reached the top of my climb, it was important to sit and enjoy the view.

Coming Home

It's my Uncle Tom's 84th birthday and my siblings, nieces, and I are celebrating by taking him out to dinner at the Drake Diner, a neat spot in the Drake University neighborhood.

I rise when he hobbles through the door that leads to the patio. Uncle Tom is a tall man, over 6 foot, and he relies heavily on his cane. He slowly eases into the chair next to me at the head of the table. Conversation during the large family gathering starts and stops like traffic in a construction zone.

But I'm not here. I'm at the top of Angel's Dead End at Loess Hills feeling the touch of a gentle breeze caress my cheek. I'm at Palisades-Kepler State Park snuggled in my sleeping bag, the rain hammering my tent and the thunder grumbling around me. I'm at the Effigy Mounds, my feet treading lightly among its silent, sacred mounds.

I return to the conversation when my uncle asks me who the people are at the other end of the table. I tell him they're his great nieces, Sarah and Brianne. Sadly, he is showing signs of early dementia.

I am so glad that I did this adventure now. Who knows where I will be in another year. Five years?

I think of how at peace I am with myself and my life, at last. I'm surrounded by my loving family. I am home, where I belong.

I hear a buzzing near my ear. That annoying pest, *Low Self-Worth*, which trailed me throughout my career, lands on my arm. I give it a quick slap and then flick it away with my middle finger.

I win.